178

THE ART AND THOUGHT

OF

MICHELANGELO

THE ART AND THOUGHT
OF
MICHELANGELO

BY

CHARLES DE TOLNAY

TRANSLATED FROM THE FRENCH BY

NAN BURANELLI

PANTHEON BOOKS

A DIVISION OF RANDOM HOUSE

NEW YORK

The photographs in this book are reproduced with the kind permission of the following:

Fotografie Alinari-Anderson-Brogi, Florence (Permission from Art Reference Bureau, Ancram, New York)
The Ashmolean Museum, Oxford
Dr. Lorenzo Del Turco, Rome
Enciclopedia dell'Arte, Rome
The Fogg Art Museum, Harvard University
Photographie Giraudon, Paris

FIRST PRINTING

Library of Congress catalog card number: 64–10979

Originally published in German as WERK UND WELTBILD DES MICHELANGELO. Copyright 1949 by Rhein-Verlag A. G.

DESIGN BY VINCENT TORRE

Contents

Contents

Illustrations

[after page 146]

(vii)

Illustrations

Illustrations

Illustrations

Introduction

THIS small volume presents a survey of Michelangelo's ideas as they are revealed in his writings and in his artistic works. A discussion of Michelangelo's political, philosophical, religious, and aesthetic concepts is quite clearly a schematization that can be justified only methodologically. It is always the same world of his thought. Even when one aspect predominates, the other aspects are also present.

Michelangelo's thought never shows any tendency to coalesce into a coherent and closed system, but rather remains linked to his personality and to his mental and moral development. His ideas, taken as a whole, have an organic rather than a systematic character. Since the master incorporated many of his thoughts into his sculpture and painting, these ideas are perceptible through their material forms. The difficulties of interpretation which stem from this are not insurmountable, for the master's letters and poems offer sufficient documentation to confirm the analysis attempted here mainly from a study of his plastic creations.

Introduction

The present book is based on four lectures delivered by the author in 1948 at the Collège de France, under the title *L'Art et la Pensée de Michel-Ange*. These were published in a German translation (Zurich, 1948) under the title: *Werk und Weltbild des Michelangelo*. The original text remains essentially unchanged; the notes have been augmented to include recent bibliography. Illustrations have been added.

The first part of the original preface is reprinted at the end of the book.

THE ART AND
THOUGHT
OF
MICHELANGELO

CHAPTER

I

Michelangelo's Political Opinions

ALTHOUGH Michelangelo's biographers attach great importance to his behavior before, during, and after the siege of Florence in 1529–30, his political opinions have not yet, so far as I know, been dealt with comprehensively. His behavior is regarded by some as proof of his great Italian patriotism, of his republicanism, of his violent hostility toward the Medici—and he is cast in the mold of a national hero. This was the view mainly held by the Italian writers during the period of Romanticism.[1] Others have seen the flight of 1529 as a betrayal of weakness and a morally reprehensible display of cowardice. This was the opinion of writers during the period of Positivism.[2]

In fact Michelangelo, even though he was a Florentine republican, never repudiated the Medici. He grew up under the patronage of Lorenzo de' Medici, and he served the two

Medici popes, Leo X and Clement VII, in turn. He was a republican, but his notion of freedom did not apply to the *popolani,* the lower orders, who were, in his opinion, inferior to the free citizens, those who paid taxes (*gravezze*).[3] We know from his letters that he was proud of belonging to a family that had paid taxes to Florence for three hundred years. The modern idea of universal freedom was quite foreign to him, although his contemporary Francesco Vettori had a clear understanding of it. Furthermore he was an aristocrat, and proud of his noble birth, seeing in it a special virtue.[4] All of which means that Michelangelo's political attitudes cannot be understood according to modern ideas. They were dictated not so much by reason and interest as by feeling and instinct. They bring to mind the Florentines of the medieval Commune, whose ideal citizen was derived from the Ciceronian idea of the Roman citizen. Just as Michelangelo's art was inspired not by the art of his time but by that of Giotto, Masaccio, Donatello, and Quercia (the first of whom lived two centuries before him, the others one century), so was he closer in political feeling to such old Republicans of Florence as Leonardo Bruni and Matteo Palmieri than to his contemporaries Machiavelli and Guicciardini. He knew Machiavelli personally, as recent research has shown,[5] but he could not have been affected by his political science, based as it was on practical experience and not influenced by ethics.[6] Unlike Machiavelli, Michelangelo does not seem to have been acquainted with the idea of the Italian nation, an idea which had nevertheless existed since the time of Dante (*Purgatorio* VI, 6 f.) and Petrarch and had been analyzed by Machiavelli. Michelangelo's fatherland (*patria*) was the free city-state of Florence. His political thought was dictated by his love for his city. Florence was to him a living being; he called it his "nurse" (*nutrice*), or his "nest," a term

(4)

already used by Dante, the *nido* in which he was born and which he always loved with filial devotion.[7] He always wanted to be buried in Florence, a wish which he expressed several times to his nephew Lionardo and to his pupil Daniele da Volterra.[8]

His political views cannot be dissociated from his attachment to Florence—this living countryside, this human community, this work of art. He felt in his youth and in his mature years what we would call today a "local patriotism," although the term had a much broader meaning then than it has now: for the man of the Middle Ages and of the early Renaissance, his native city was the whole world. There was no sterner punishment than exile. Dante, throughout his life of exile, far from his city, thought only of Florence. Speaking from his poignant memories of his city (*Paradiso* XXV, 5), he movingly called it the "bello ovile ovi' io dormi' agnello": "that lovely cradle where I slept like a lamb."

It was only toward the end of his life that Michelangelo reached a more universal conception; he became a citizen of Christendom. That intermediary between the two extremes of local and universal which constitutes modern "patriotism" was absent from his thought.

At first he showed only an instinctive love of Florence, and this did not manifest itself until he left his birthplace. It was probably during his stay in Venice and Bologna (1494), and in the course of his years in Rome (1496–1501), that he became aware of the love he bore Florence.[9] He was devoured by homesickness. If this was not yet a political attitude, it was the germ which would grow until it produced the citizen and patriot. This instinctive love developed into a conscious attitude only when he was faced with a concrete artistic task. The commission for a *David* forced him to define and clarify his conception of the civic virtues. The ideas thus conceived, during the execution of a work of art, expanded later into moral maxims, into firm convictions, and determined his actions before and during the siege of Florence (1529–30).

During the reign of Lorenzo the Magnificent, and during Savonarola's Republic and the years in Rome (1496–1501), Michelangelo evidently did not have a clear-cut attitude, politically speaking. No doubt, coming as he did from an old Guelph family, he already had republican inclinations, but because he was a protégé of Lorenzo the Magnificent, he shunned political and social movements; he took no part in the struggles between the factions of the *popolo grasso* and the *popolo minuto,* the *arti maggiori* and the *arti minori;* and he did not feel any necessity to define his position.

The moment for that came with the new constitution of the Florentine Republic in 1501, and with the election of his friend Piero Soderini as the first Gonfaloniere for life. The new Republic, unlike the preceding one (Savonarola's), cherished the youthful master. During the first years of this Republic, Michelangelo was overwhelmed with commissions from the Signoria and the ancient guilds of the city, which were still very powerful.[10] He tried to incorporate the civic virtues, those pillars of the republican regime, into some of his works, and in this way to serve the new Republic which appreciated him as an artist.

Michelangelo was commissioned to execute the *David* on August 16, 1501, twelve days after the adoption of the new constitution. It was perhaps the latter event that gave the young master the idea of treating David, not as a biblical hero, but as the defender and the just administrator of his people, an example set before the Florentines to inspire them to defend the Republic and govern it justly. He carved the giant work from a single block of marble originally intended to crown one of the buttresses of the Florentine Cathedral; the block had been roughhewn forty years before by Agostino di

(6)

PLATE VIII

Duccio, who mutilated it and was therefore unable to finish it. Michelangelo was able to carve it, without any additions, and finished it by the beginning of 1504.[11]

Florence already owned several Davids: the celebrated statues by Donatello and Verrocchio, a number of little bronze statuettes, and a fresco by Michelangelo's master, Domenico Ghirlandaio, in Santa Trinità above the Cappella Sassetti. All of them show the biblical child, sword in hand, one foot on Goliath's head, wearing either a timid expression, with head slightly bowed, or else the proud smile of victory. Ghirlandaio even made an attempt to connect David directly with the Sassetti family by putting in one hand a sling with a stone, which was an emblem of the family, and in the other a shield with the Sassetti coat of arms. The contrapostal pose already anticipated Michelangelo's David.[12]

Michelangelo's David is different: he is an adolescent, naked, bereft of the traditional attributes—such as the sword or Goliath's head—retaining only the sling, and even that hidden behind his back. Instead of following the traditional Davids of the fifteenth century, Michelangelo's David is closer in type to the antique Hercules.[13] The position of the limbs and head, the complete nudity of the figure, and the contrasted movement of the arms in opposite directions are all to be found in the sculptured figures of Hercules on ancient sarcophagi. Unlike his predecessors, Michelangelo doesn't seem to be trying to show us a precise moment in the life of David. He wants above all to emphasize the permanent features of David's character and his moral attitude. We have here an incarnation of moral and physical strength which knows no fear and is ready to defend an ideal.

This slender, muscular body reveals no slackening of energy but rather an alertness, a dynamism of potential power. Outwardly he seems to be self-possessed and calm; inwardly he is taut and ready for action. Anger and heroic scorn are

(7)

PLATE XLVII

written on his noble face. Under the thick shock of hair like tongues of flame and the stormy furrows of a brow frowning in indignation, we encounter the fire of a glance full of pride and disdain. The eyelids are contracted, the nostrils pinched with rage, the lips swollen with anger. He is the embodiment of *fortezza* (force) and *ira* (anger). The Florentine humanists of the early Renaissance considered *fortezza* to be the greatest of the civic virtues. From the second quarter of the fifteenth century on, and in contrast to the stoic tradition of Cicero, which placed philosophy and diplomacy above arms, they had exalted the active struggle in defense of the homeland. This doctrine of *fortezza,* praised as a civic virtue, was associated by Renaissance writers (the Florentines first and after them those from the rest of Italy) with the doctrine of *ira,* the passion of anger, which had been condemned as a vice in the Middle Ages, until it too was raised by them to the rank of a civic virtue. According to Coluccio Salutati, anger is a vice only if it affects the judgment; when it arouses the courage of the citizen in the struggle for liberty it becomes a virtue. It is anger which heightens the moral force of the brave man; and Leonardo Bruni tells us that *fortitudo* and *pietas*, the two virtues of strength and love of country, are engendered only by *ira*. Palmieri (*Vita civile,* ed. 1830, p. 81) explains that anger can sustain *fortezza*, since it causes man to choose danger for virtue's sake.[14] Landino, too, at the end of the century, finds in Platonism a justification of anger in terms of virtue.

Therefore Michelangelo's David is an embodiment of the two chief civic virtues of the Renaissance. Michelangelo identified him with the Hercules type in order to better express *fortezza.* Just as one was the symbol of strength for classical antiquity, so the other was the *manu fortis* of the Middle Ages. It is not surprising that Michelangelo merged the two in a monument destined to exalt the civic virtues; and all the more

(8)

PLATE XXIII

because, from the end of the thirteenth century, Hercules had been honored as the patron and protector of Florence.

The Commune of Florence in the Middle Ages armed its free citizens; this custom was abolished by the Medici, who disarmed the people. In humanist writings of the beginning of the fifteenth century, such as those of Leonardo Bruni, the idea of a fighting militia reappeared along with the ideal of the citizen warrior defending liberty.[15] Donatello's *St. George*, originally at Or San Michele and now in the Bargello, is an early incarnation of this citizen warrior, which explains its inner similarity to Michelangelo's *David*. This is also the idea that Machiavelli expressed when he said in his *Principe* (Book XII): "È necessario d'armasi d'arme proprie e d'uomini suoi propri . . ." (It is necessary to arm oneself with one's own arms and with one's own men [that is, no more mercenaries]). Piero Soderini, on the advice of Machiavelli (who was at that time secretary to the second chancellery), created the city militia. This was one of the main points in the reform of the city's constitution. Machiavelli's ideas were anticipated by about five years in Michelangelo's David, the embodiment of the ideal of the *cittadino guerriero*.

There is a sentence in Vasari which confirms this interpretation and shows that the statue was already regarded by Michelangelo's contemporaries as the representation of a republican political idea. He says: "Si come egli haveva difeso il suo popolo e governatolo con giustizia, così chi governava quella città dovesse animosamente difenderla e giustamente governarla." (Just as he [David] defended his people and governed them with justice, in the same way whoever rules this city [Florence] should defend it courageously and govern it justly.)

Another argument supporting the theory of the political significance of the statue is to be found in the chronicles of Landucci, from which we learn that on the night of May 14,

(9)

PLATE XLVII

1504, while preparations were being made to transport the statue from the Opera del Duomo, where Michelangelo had finished it, to its permanent resting place before the entrance of the Palazzo della Signoria, it was attacked with stones, and guards had to be posted to protect it. How can this attack against a work of art be explained, unless we recognize that it must have had political significance? It was only natural that the Medici party would want to destroy this symbol of its enemy, the Republic. Furthermore, on April 26, 1527, during riots which took place around the Palazzo della Signoria following a new expulsion of the Medici, a bench was thrown from a window of the palace at the *David* and broke its left arm (Vasari, 1568, p. 386); this second outrage can probably be explained in the same way as the first.

The choice of location for the statue beside the entrance door to the Palazzo della Signoria further confirms this interpretation. A committee, consisting for the most part of well-known artists, Florentine notables, and artisans, was formed at the request of the Consoli dell' Arte della Lana and of Michelangelo in January 1504, shortly before the statue was finished, for the express purpose of suggesting a fitting location for the *David*. Michelangelo himself was not present at the meeting. Nevertheless it is possible to deduce his opinion indirectly from the minutes.

The proposal to put the statue on the *ringhiera,* to the left of the main entrance of the Palazzo della Signoria and in the axis of the tower, in place of Donatello's *Judith,* was made and defended by only one individual, Francesco, the first Herald of Florence; and even he suggested the center of the courtyard as an alternative, although he would have preferred to see the *David* in the *Judith*'s place. For this preference he offered the curious argument that the *Judith* was of ill omen (*segno mortifero*): she had been installed under an ill-fated star and had brought only bad luck to Florence. He added that the emblems (*insegna*) of the city were the lily and the cross, and not Judith; and that consequently she should not be allowed to remain on that spot.

Although Herald Francesco was the only one to hold this opinion, it prevailed. The most plausible explanation of this fact is that the artist himself wanted to have his work installed there. The opinion of Salvestro, a jeweler, seems to confirm this theory. He said in effect that the statue had to be placed close to the palace, "intorno al palazzo," "because he who had created it knew better than anyone else where it should be put." Two artists of high repute, Filippino Lippi and Piero di Cosimo, concurred in this view.[16]

The fact is that Michelangelo was anxious to see his *David* installed in this precise place because of the political significance of the statue. Donatello had executed the Judith group for Cosimo de' Medici, and at first the work had been kept in the palace belonging to that family. Shortly after the expulsion of the Medici in 1494 the citizens of Florence had decided to move the statue to the front of the Palazzo della Signoria, and they endowed the change with a political significance, viewing the statue as a symbol of the city-state's victory over its tyrants. The following device was engraved on the new pedestal: "Exemplum salutis publicae cives posuere 1495." From that date on, the place commemorated the victory of civil liberties and the defeat of tyrants. It was precisely this idea of the defense of republican liberties that Michelangelo intended to express, in a grander and nobler way, in his *David*.[17]

This was not the only David that Michelangelo did at this time. During the summer of 1502 the Signoria commissioned him to execute a second David in bronze, as a gift for Pierre de Rohan, Maréchal de Gié, who was then in the service of Francis I. Alliance with the King of France was an old Guelph political tradition; and the Signoria had everything to gain from being on good terms with a Marshal of France.

The statue has been lost; but there is a sketch of it by Michelangelo in the Louvre.[18] Because the Marshal so wished, the statue was to be similar to the one in the courtyard of the Palazzo della Signoria, that is, the bronze *David* by Donatello. So Michelangelo followed Donatello's conception in its general outline. This David is an adolescent, his head slightly inclined, his sword in one hand, his sling in the other which is resting on his hip; and his clawlike foot is crushing Goliath's head. But the bearing of the figure is marked by a savage energy which is lacking in Donatello's David. The toes are clenched in his enemy's mane of hair, his muscular body seems to be filled with vibrant life and the intoxication of victory. Vitality seems to surge tumultuously within him, endlessly renewing itself and preparing for further battle. This is not David after his victory (Donatello) but David the eternal conqueror —meant perhaps as an augury for Marshal de Gié.

The government of the Florentine Republic wished to erect in front of the Palazzo della Signoria, as a companion piece to the marble *David,* a second huge statue by Michelangelo, representing Hercules and Antaeus;[19] because, as Vasari points out, both David and Hercules were emblems of the Palace. Since the Middle Ages Hercules had been considered the protector of Florence. From the end of the thirteenth century, he was portrayed as such on the seals of the city. The inscription on these seals gives his symbolic significance: "Herculaea clava domat Fiorentia prava" (With Hercules' club Florence curbs infamy), meaning that Hercules defends liberty against the domestic enemy just as David defends liberty against the foreign enemy. Michelangelo was evidently very anxious to carry out this task for the city Republic, and made every effort to procure the commission for himself when his right to it was contested. The commission was taken from him in the end and handed over to his avowed enemy, Bandinelli. This final decision was the last chapter in a strug-

PLATE XXXVIII

gle between two political powers—the Republic of Florence and the Medici—which spanned a quarter of a century.

The Medici were anxious to prevent the sovereignty of the Florentine Republic from being symbolized by its greatest son, Michelangelo. Perhaps they realized that this statue threatened to become, in the eyes of the Florentine people, a declaration in marble of republican liberties. At the same time they must have reasoned that it would not be a very clever move to forbid completely the erection of a Hercules in front of the Palazzo della Signoria and to oppose the will of the people. A compromise appeared desirable. They permitted the execution of the monument not by Michelangelo, who was a republican, but by Bandinelli, an artist who was detested in the town and well known as an opportunist. The Medici no doubt reasoned that a Hercules by Bandinelli would present no threat to them. This decision, which gave Bandinelli the commission after the fall of the last Florentine Republic, was at the same time a witness to the victory of the Medici over the will of the people of Florence.

The project was first mentioned in letters written by Piero Soderini in 1508. These letters show that the idea for the group came from the republican government of the city. Michelangelo could not accept the commission at that time because Julius II, in whose service he then was, had refused him permission to leave Bologna. The block was roughhewn at Carrara about 1515, and Michelangelo, in order to get the commission, tried to win the favor of Leo X. But the Pope, who was a Medici, gave it to Bandinelli. Litigation began in 1529. Clement VII, also a Medici, who was Pope at the time, insisted that the block be executed by Bandinelli, whereas the Signoria took Michelangelo's part and declared it to be "the general desire of the Florentine people" that Michelangelo should make the statue. The latter then offered to do the work gratuitously for the Signoria if the Pope would free him to devote himself to it. The Pope refused him permission and insisted that Michelangelo finish the tomb of Julius II and, apart from this, work exclusively for him. After the expulsion of the Medici, the government of the last Republic decreed in 1528 that the block, already half done by Bandinelli, should be delivered to Michelangelo with the proviso that he make two figures out of it, as he saw fit. According to Vasari, Michelangelo decided at this point to make a Samson with two Philistines instead of the Hercules. (The composition is known only from copies.) When the Republic fell, Clement VII took possession of the block once more and gave it back to Bandinelli, who finally finished the group of Hercules and Cacus in 1534. It still stands beside the entrance of the Palazzo, balancing the *David*.

All we have left of Michelangelo's plans for the Hercules and Antaeus group are three masterly sketches in red chalk done about 1525.[20] They show Hercules capturing Antaeus. Antaeus is trying to escape from his grasp and the two bodies are intertwined in a spiral. Hercules cannot get rid of his antagonist; he dominates him without destroying him. These are mortal enemies. Michelangelo portrays not a transitory moment but a permanent struggle, and perhaps he means to say here that the inner enemy is always present, that he must continually be kept subdued. But this is only conjecture.

Another important commission which the government of the Republic gave Michelangelo was the commemoration of the victory of Florence over Pisa by a fresco representing the Battle of Cascina. Michelangelo was to execute this fresco in the great Council Hall of the Signoria. It was a high honor for for the young artist. He was entering into direct competition with the illustrious Leonardo da Vinci, who the year before had been commissioned to decorate the Hall. Michelangelo worked on the preliminary cartoon with some interruptions until 1506, but never succeeded in actually executing the

(14)

PLATE XXXVIII

fresco. Vasari says that Bastiano da Sangallo's copy, which is now preserved in Holkham (Lord Leicester), gives an exact reproduction of the whole composition. The theme was topical. The Florentines, at war with Pisa in the summer of 1504, had sacked the town. They had seized the ships used to carry grain to Pisa. These events just preceded the commission of Michelangelo, in August 1504, to commemorate the Florentines' greatest victory over the Pisans at Cascina in 1364. Perhaps the magistrates thought of this fresco as a good omen for future victories over Pisa.

Contrary to tradition, Michelangelo did not portray the battle itself. He chose an episode related in the chronicles of Filippo Villani, according to which the leader of the Florentine army had established his camp outside Cascina, on the Arno. It was hot and some soldiers, having taken off their breastplates, were stretched out on the bank; others were bathing in the river. The camp was unprotected, the captain taking no account of the proximity of the Pisans. Understanding the imminent danger, Manno Donati, one of the soldiers, cried out: "We are lost!" and begged the captain to organize an immediate defense—a piece of foresight which saved the Florentines. Probably Michelangelo chose this moment, rather than the battle itself, to remind his fellow citizens of the necessity for constant preparation and determined vigilance.

He never executed this fresco. The fate of the cartoon was rather like that of the Hercules block. The cartoon was displayed at first in the Council Hall for which the fresco was destined. But about 1512, when the Medici regained power, this republican symbol was transferred to the Hall of the Popes, near Santa Maria Novella, by Leo X, who was a Medici pope. From there the cartoon was taken to the Medici palace itself, where it was cut into pieces. Vasari in his first edition maintained that several artists were to blame for this vandalism. In his second edition he said that Bandinelli destroyed

(15)

PLATE V

the work in 1512, the year in which the Republic fell. Bandinelli, favorite of the Medici and enemy of Michelangelo and
the Republic, could very well have been the perpetrator of
this crime at the time of the Medici's return to power.[21]

After the sack of Rome in 1527, the leaders of the Medici
faction were obliged to leave the city once more, and the republican regime, which had been interrupted by the Medici
fifteen years earlier in 1512, was restored. This was the last
Republic of Florence. During the three years of its existence,
from 1527 to 1530, Michelangelo was to put into practice
the opinions on the virtues and duties of a citizen which he
symbolized in the *David*, the Hercules and Antaeus sketches,
and the *Battle of Cascina*. It is worth noting that Michelangelo
not only worked as an artist for the last Republic (Hercules
group) but contributed directly to its military defense. He
worked on the fortifications of the city in order to satisfy his
political principles, which demanded of each citizen a
contribution to the defense of his country. In the autumn of
1528 he decided to offer his services as an expert on fortifications, "gratis e amorevolmente" (Gaye, II, p. 62). The problem
was one of completing and improving upon the fortifications
begun by the Medici in 1525–26. In January 1529, Michelangelo became a member of the Nove della Milizia (the Commission on Fortifications). In April 1529, he was named head
of the Dieci della Guerra (the supreme council of war), with
the title of "Governatore e procuratore generale sopra alla
fabbrica e fortificazione delle mura della città di Firenze." The
nomination document (Gotti, II, p. 62) says expressly that
the Signori dei Dieci della Guerra, "having considered the
qualifications of a large number of well-known architects in
this field [*scil*. the building of fortifications] to execute the
fortifications now necessary for the city, in view of the virtue
and training of our citizen Michelangelo, and knowing to
what degree he excells in architecture (not to mention his ex-

ceptional qualities as regards the other liberal arts), and knowing that in the universal opinion of men there is no one superior to him today; and inasmuch as he is also the peer of every good and devoted citizen in his love and affection for his country, have finally made the decision to employ his talents." So he was named "Governatore" for a year, with an indemnity of a "fiorino d'oro" a day. Let us remember that he had, until then, served the Republic without recompense.[22]

Michelangelo seems to have taken to the task with enthusiasm and even ardor. He drew a series of magnificent large plans for the fortifications of the walls and gates of Florence (Casa Buonarroti, Florence). These plans, by their originality and ingenuity, marked a decisive point in the history of the architecture of fortification, and were much admired by the great masters of fortification of the seventeenth century, such as Vauban. From a practical point of view they were much more effective than the earlier works of fortification; by means of diagonal and curved walls Michelangelo devised a system which ensured that the artillery fire of a besieging army could only attack the walls obliquely. In this way he avoided the destructive effect of a battery of gunfire aimed directly at the walls; further, by an ingenious disposition of bastions he created centers of attack from which to repulse the enemy. Apart from their practical qualities, these designs also have artistic beauty; conceived as they were by a sculptor's imagination, they have the organic character of living creatures, and look rather like the silhouettes of crustaceans, with their long antennae.[23]

These splendid plans were not accepted by the Gonfaloniere Niccolò Capponi (Busini, p. 103). After Capponi's dismissal, his successor, Carducci, found Michelangelo "troppo timido et sospettoso," when the latter, who had a premonition of the treachery of Malatesta Baglioni, notified the Signoria of suspicions which a year later proved to be well founded. Foreseeing the danger which was threatening the city (the Peace of Barcelona in June 1529 brought about the alliance of Charles V and Clement VII, and Florence was promised to the Medici Pope), and aware on the other hand of the lack of success in all his attempts to warn the magistrates of disaster, Michelangelo, in a moment of panic, suddenly and "molto disordinatamente" took flight in September of 1529—according to a letter by Paesano (J. A. Symonds, *Life of Michelangelo*, London [1893], p. 423), "per fuggire il fastidio et ancora la mala fortuna della guerra."

He went to Venice by way of Ferrara, and still not feeling safe, thought of fleeing to France. This episode took place about three weeks *before* the onset of the siege by the combined armies of the Pope and the Emperor (the siege began on October 10, 1529). For a proper understanding of Michelangelo's conduct it seems important to stress this chronological fact, and also Michelangelo's message to the Signoria, three days after the beginning of the siege. The master let it be known then that he was ready to return to Florence on condition that he would be pardoned. He did indeed return toward the end of November, at a time when all the southern part of the town was already besieged. Since Michelangelo was coming from Venice, he was able to enter by one of the northern gates of Florence, where communications had not yet been cut by the enemy.

One of the main factors influencing this decision to return was probably the series of eleven letters which he received while in Venice from his Florentine friends; one in particular from Giovanni Battista della Palla seems to have played an important part in the decision. It also demonstrates the ardent patriotism of the Florentines: "All your friends, without a single dissenting voice, unhesitatingly, unanimously, exhort you to come back and save your life, your country, your friends, your goods, and your honor, and enjoy the new era which you have so ardently desired and hoped for." [24] The last sentence alludes no doubt to previous conversations between the friends about the Republic. This letter from della Palla overflows with optimism: he never doubted that victory would be theirs, and believed in the coming of a golden age for Florence. The same spirit of patriotism and courage manifests itself in other documents of this period; for example, the report of Carlo Cappello, the Venetian ambassador in Florence (Gotti, I, p. 198) and the letter from the Balia of Florence (Gaye, II, p. 211) to the Florentine ambassador in Venice: "Siamo disposti a mettervi tutte le nostre facultà prima che venire sotto il giogo della tirannide." "E certamente meritano i nostri cittadini grandissima commendatione . . . non è grave peso [*scil*. per i nostri cittadini] per mantenere questa libertà, la dolcezza della quale tanto più si gusta, quanto maggiore è la guerra che gli è fatta." (We are disposed to use all our strength [to defend the city], before we fall under the yoke of tyranny . . . Certainly our citizens merit the greatest praise . . . It is not a heavy burden [for our citizens] to maintain their liberty, the sweetness of which they enjoy all the more the stronger the assault made upon it.)

It was to this Florence, besieged but full of hope and courage, that Michelangelo returned. He was first punished by the Consiglio Maggiore for his flight, but the punishment was not severe. From then on he bore himself courageously in the besieged city. However, we know very little about his life during this period. He transformed into an artillery post the bastions and the tower of San Miniato (Condivi; Vasari; Varchi, *Storia* II, 34). On February 22, 1530, he received permission to climb up onto the dome of the Cathedral, probably to obtain a bird's-eye view of the positions of the besieging troops (Gotti, I, p. 197). These facts speak clearly. His flight three weeks *before* the siege was counteracted by his return in the middle of the critical period, as well as by the way in which he conducted himself, both before the flight and after his return, in his capacity as architect of the fortifications.

After the capitulation of Florence, on August 12, 1530, Michelangelo hid at first in order to avoid the vengeance of the city's conquerors. But he was soon pardoned by Clement VII because of his status as a famous artist, and he had no alternative but to place himself at the disposition of the city's new masters. He resumed his work on the Medici Chapel at the same time that he was obliged to execute works for the greatest enemies of Florentine liberty, which must have been supremely humiliating for him. The works in question were a David or Apollo ordered by the cruel Baccio Valori, the Pope's Commissary, and a cartoon representing *Noli me tangere* for the Marchese del Vasto, one of the commanders of the imperial armies.[25]

These two works seem to express Michelangelo's true feelings in an indirect way. Under the right foot of the statue, which is sometimes called *Apollo* and sometimes *David*, can be seen a roughly sketched round shape, doubtless the head of Goliath. David is holding the sling in his left hand, the stone in his right. Instead of having a normal *contrapposto* position based on the laws of gravity, the figure seems to live in a dream world. Its gestures are unconscious reflections of the life of the soul, like the gestures of a man in a dream who, with face turned sideways and eyes half open, is trying to rid himself of a nightmare. This David is not the personification of *fortezza* or of the eternal conqueror, but of a conqueror who is troubled by his victory and would seem to be haunted by his conscience. One wonders if Michelangelo, in making this strange dreaming David, did not mean to point out to the new conqueror, Baccio Valori, that every victory is not a triumph. Perhaps this is why his contemporaries were so ambiguous about the name of the statue, which they some-

(20)

PLATE XIII

times called *David* and sometimes *Apollo*. Had they called it *David* only, the allusion would have been too obvious.

The other work which Michelangelo was obliged to execute at the order of an enemy of the Republic, this time the Marchese del Vasto, was a cartoon representing *Noli me tangere*. Here perhaps the intention may have been to point out that occupied Florence must not be soiled by sacrilegious hands. The cartoon is lost. Two of the copies in Florence and Milan, both attributed to Pontormo, show in the background a view of the walls of a city—perhaps the walls of Florence.

After Michelangelo's final departure from Florence in 1534, during the voluntary exile which filled the last thirty years of his life, he remained faithful to the political ideals of his youth. Before we discuss in detail the evidence of this fidelity, the reasons for the "exile," after the death of Clement VII in September of 1534, should be examined.[26]

In several letters of 1555 and 1557, the artist gave as the reason for his absence from Florence his position as chief architect of St. Peter's, saying that he could not abandon the "fabbrica di San Pietro" without committing a great sin, that such an act would put all Christianity to shame: "Sarebemi grandissima vergogna in tutta la Cristianità, e a l'animo grandissimo peccato" (Milanesi, pp. 537–38). But there were certainly other reasons, above all the fact that as an old republican he felt himself personally affected by the transformation of Florence into a duchy, which he regarded as a kind of bondage for his city. He did not want to live in a Florence completely under the heel of the Medici. It should not be forgotten that earlier, under Lorenzo de' Medici, the republican institutions had to all appearances been respected; and that the young Michelangelo was unable, as were his contemporaries, to see through this very well camouflaged tyranny. He never openly referred in his letters to the political reason for his exile, but there is existing evidence which leaves little room for doubt: the bust of Brutus, the madrigal on tyranny, the epigram on the *Notte,* and the letter from del Riccio to Francis I about the execution of an equestrian statue.

During his long stay in Rome, Michelangelo remained in touch with a large number of exiled Florentines, among them "suo amicissimo" Donato Giannotti, the historian, who was Secretary of State at the time of the last Florentine Republic, as Machiavelli had been before him, and who, in exile, fought with his pen for the liberty of the Republic against its tyrants. Giannotti entered the service of another Florentine exile, Cardinal Niccolò Ridolfi, whose secretary he became. Michelangelo no doubt talked over the tragic fate of their city with Giannotti; it is highly probable that they discussed the problem of tyrannicide. In several of his works Giannotti dealt with this question and sided with the tyrannicides, particularly in the case of Brutus and Cassius. He reproached Dante with having put them in Hell: "Io li vorrei collocare nella più honorata parte del Paradiso." In the Middle Ages, in Dante's time (*Inferno* XXXIV, 64; *Paradiso* VI, 74), Brutus was condemned not only for the murder of his benefactor Caesar but also for having killed in Caesar the restorer of world peace and the founder of the Imperium Romanum, which was then considered identical with the Christian Roman Empire. Boccaccio was one of the first to show signs of a change of opinion on this point: "Non vi è sacrificio più accetto, del sangue di un tiranno" (*De casibus virorum illustrium,* II, 15). During the Renaissance a veritable cult of Brutus grew up, and concurrently the Roman Empire was regarded as the beginning of the decadence of Rome. Brutus was extolled as an ideal and an example each time the Florentines tried to get rid of the

Medici. Every Florentine who had killed or tried to kill a Medici was acclaimed as a "nuovo Bruto." Cola Montano, Pietro Paolo Boscoli, Rinuccini, and Lorenzino de' Medici (the assassin of Alessandro de' Medici) were lauded in this way.

There is in the Bargello a bust by Michelangelo representing Brutus which, according to Vasari, was executed at the request of Messer Donato Giannotti for Cardinal Niccolò Ridolfi; so it was Giannotti who inspired the bust. The exact date of its execution is not known. The date of Giannotti's entry into the Cardinal's service in 1539 offers a *terminus post quem*. Stylistically the head of Brutus is related to the figures in the *Last Judgment* (especially those to the right of Christ). From this the approximate date of the work can be deduced to be 1539–40. This bust is important to an understanding of the master's political convictions.[27]

The thick, strong neck—almost a bull's neck—is surmounted by a relatively small head with an almost rectangular profile, a low flat brow, a nose drawn in severe straight lines, a tightly closed mouth, and an angular jutting chin. These simplified features are framed by hair which is rough-hewn and covers the whole cranium like a cap. The head, turned to the left, is seen first in full profile. The expression seems to be one of calm; but a closer examination reveals anger there, disdain and bitter scorn, controlled with effort by an extraordinary act of will. These passions can be read in the slightly frowning eyebrows, the wrinkles around the mouth, the dilated nostrils, and the sideward glance. It is important to notice that the two halves of the face are asymmetrical: the right side (to the statue's right) is calm but tense; the left side is more dramatic and openly reveals the passions which animate it. According to a conception of the Middle Ages the right side is protected by God, the left side is open to evil; according to modern psychology the right side of the face is the mirror of man's inner life and the left side

(23)

PLATE XXVI

that of his social life. All realist art, whether consciously or not, has reproduced this asymmetry of the human face which is a general law; but Michelangelo seems to have been the first to use the external phenomenon deliberately to indicate the inner forces which constitute the *causa efficiens* of the asymmetry.

There is no preliminary drawing of the Brutus still in existence; but a "preliminary study" of the bust itself exists in the little profile relief on the fibula. Since this detail is almost invisible to the viewer because of its position, it may be surmised that Michelangelo executed it for himself, more or less as a preparatory study. The head, with its bare neck, is in the same pose as the heads of Brutus on ancient coins; the features resemble those of the bust, with the difference that the fibula profile, in the individuality of its details, seems to be a portrait, while the bust has a more generalized character. This demonstrates Michelangelo's procedure: starting with a concrete portrait, he ends by creating a type inspired by ancient Caracalla busts. We can only speculate about the identity of the model on the fibula. It could not have been Lorenzino de' Medici, for there is no resemblance to him. It would be natural to suppose that it was a portrait of the Maecenas, Cardinal Ridolfi; but there again there is no resemblance. This leaves the conjecture that it is a portrait of Giannotti. As no portrait of the latter exists, this cannot be verified.

Michelangelo's conception of Brutus is clearly expressed in this bust: he represents heroic disdain—obviously for those who would destroy liberty. This point of view occurs again in the *Dialogues* by Donato Giannotti: "De' giorni che Dante consumò nell' cercare l'Inferno e'l Purgatorio." [28] Here, Michelangelo and Giannotti debate whether Dante was right or wrong to send Brutus and Cassius to Hell. Giannotti declares himself to be completely opposed to Dante; Michelangelo tries to justify both Dante and Brutus, with arguments which

(24)

PLATE XXVI

savor of sophism and tend to contradict themselves. Obviously one cannot be sure that this dialogue really took place, but it is hardly credible that it was made up out of nothing.[29] It testifies to Michelangelo's love and veneration for Dante and to his fidelity to his political ideal, for he says: "He who kills a tyrant kills not a man but a wild beast in man's form . . . so Brutus and Cassius did not sin in killing Caesar" (p. 93). The arguments where Michelangelo tries to justify Dante are only of secondary importance to our problem, which is that of Michelangelo's attitude to tyrannicide.

A madrigal by Michelangelo, of the same period as Giannotti's *Dialogue*, expresses a similar view of tyranny. In this madrigal (Frey, *Dicht*. CIX, 48) Florence, in the form of a beautiful woman, addresses herself to the Florentine exiles; the latter deplore the enslavement of their land and the injustice which has been done to it, for an individual has appropriated to himself what had been created for everyone: "Un sol s'appropria quel che è dato a tanti." But Florence consoles them: "Col gran timor non gode il gran peccato . . ." (Because of the fear that overwhelms him, the tyrant cannot enjoy the fruits of his terrible sin).

Passing now from these general observations by Michelangelo on tyranny to his judgment of the events which took place in the Florence of his time, we find revealing evidence that he considered the fall of the Republic as the death of liberty, and that he saw at first in Cosimo de' Medici's accession to power the advent of a tyrant. One instance of this is the famous quatrain on the *Notte,* one of the allegorical statues in the Medici Chapel. This quatrain was probably written in 1545, for it was then that the Chapel was opened to the public. Among the numerous admirers who at that time wrote verses in honor of Michelangelo's work was a young humanist, Giovanni Strozzi, who composed an epigram praising the "dolce atti" of the figure sculptured by an Angelo, or angel (a play on the artist's name). This statue, even though it is asleep, still seems to be alive. "Waken her and talk to her, if you do not believe it," he advises the viewer. To these rather precious, artificial verses, which are utterly devoid of originality, Michelangelo replies in a quatrain of caustic comment (Frey, *Dicht.* CIX, 17):

> *Caro m'è il sonno, e più l'esser di sasso,*
> *Mentre che'l danno e la vergogna dura,*
> *Non veder, non sentir, m'è gran ventura;*
> *Però, non mi destar, deh! parla basso.*

(I enjoy being asleep, and even more being made of stone as long as shame and ruin run rife. So do not wake me, and speak softly, please.)

To be asleep, to be made of stone: these conditions liberate the mind from shame—the shame of one's country's enslavement. Originally, when Michelangelo conceived them in 1520, the Allegories of the Medici Chapel had a purely philosophical meaning: they signified Time which devours everything (cf. Michelangelo's fragment of a poem, Frey, *Dicht.* XVII, and Condivi, Vasari). The epigram on the *Notte* shows that a quarter of a century after the figure's conception, its creator injected a political meaning.[30]

The evidence assembled up to this point: the *Dialogue* by Donato Giannotti, the madrigal, and the quatrain, all date from 1545 to 1546. This, it would seem, was the moment at which Michelangelo suffered most in his feelings as a Florentine patriot. He was at that time a close friend of Luigi del Riccio, descendant of an old aristocratic Florentine family, who had been banished from the city. He was employed by Roberto Strozzi, another exile and bitter enemy of the Medici, as an agent of the Strozzi-Ulivieri bank in Rome. In June 1544, tired out by his long labors, Michelangelo fell seriously ill. Del Riccio had him taken to Roberto Strozzi's house in

Rome, surrounded him with every possible care, and as Michelangelo himself later said, "snatched him from death."

Long conversations between the master and del Riccio certainly took place. The imagination of the two republicans could hardly fail to be enflamed by talk of their city's loss of liberty.[31] On July 21, 1544, del Riccio, writing to Roberto Strozzi in Lyons, informed him of Michelangelo's gratitude, and added this touching request: "He begs you to let him have news of you and to remind the King [Francis I] of what he has already told him through Scipione and later by the courier Deo, that if the King will restore to Florence her liberty, he, Michelangelo, will erect at his own expense an equestrian statue to him on the square of the Palazzo della Signoria."

This offer has been interpreted as an indirect reproach to Francis I for having abandoned the old Franco-Florentine alliance in time of necessity, at the very moment when Charles V was helping Clement VII to besiege Florence (Dorez). But it is perhaps more plausible to see in it an attempt by Michelangelo to encourage the King of France to fulfill his traditional mission by giving Florence back her liberty. The Florentine imagination had always cherished the ideal of a "great emperor," wise and just, who would save the city. In the Middle Ages he was identified with the Germano-Roman Emperor—this is how Dante considered him; during and after the Renaissance the Capetian kings took over the role. It was always to the King of France that the Florentine Republic looked for support and alliance. Therefore, in making this moving appeal, Michelangelo was acting in the Guelph tradition: for him Francis I was the long-dreamed-of liberator. It is not known whether this offer from Michelangelo ever reached Francis I, but it is quite possible that Florentines who were exiled in France told the King about it. Michelangelo's gift to Roberto Strozzi in the same year (1544) of two marble Slaves (which are today in the Louvre), in token of his grati-

(27)

PLATE XI

tude for the hospitality he enjoyed in Strozzi's house during his illness, should not be overlooked. Strozzi presented these two magnificent figures to Francis I shortly afterwards—perhaps, as Dorez has suggested, to try and rouse him to give Florence back her independence.[32]

During the last twenty years of Michelangelo's life, his Florentine republicanism seems to have faded. The evidence concerning his attachment for Florence reveals a gradual change in this feeling. Little by little it becomes less ardent and more impersonal; the artist—an old man now—is proud only of the long pedigree of his Florentine family and of its noble origin. "Noi siamo cittadini discesi di nobilissima stirpe" (Milanesi, p. 197); "Siamo antichi cittadini fiorentini e nobili quant'è ogni altra casa" (Milanesi, p. 237; cf. also Milanesi, p. 271; Milanesi, p. 492, etc.).

In his old age, when he was about eighty, he abandoned his tenacious opposition to the new regime in Florence, a regime which ten years before had seemed to him incompatible with his republican ideals: the conflicts which had once been so violent softened with the perspective that comes with age. From 1554 on, Michelangelo even exchanged a cordial correspondence with Duke Cosimo I. And when the citizens of Florence commissioned him with plans for San Giovanni dei Fiorentini, their church in Rome, the artist accepted this task on condition that he receive "una licenza e commessione del Duca" (Milanesi, pp. 551, 552), which is to say that he now recognized the Duke as the overlord of Florence.

It would appear that in Rome in the course of the last two decades of his life, Michelangelo's Florentine patriotism slowly faded and a more universal and more spiritual ideal took form in his mind, the ideal of the citizen of the Christian world. He wanted now to act according to the postulates of "tutta la cristianità" (Milanesi, pp. 537–38; letter of 1555). His political thought became sublimated: it no longer embraced Florence alone, but all Christendom.

Two stages can be distinguished in this development of Michelangelo's thought toward universalism. The Florentine citizen passes first through the stage of citizen of the world, in the ancient Roman sense; then, he becomes a Christian. He sees in Rome a universal supranational state, *Roma aeterna,* founded by divine will and destined to exist until the end of time. This was how Dante and Petrarch also saw events; the *urbs,* the city, is the center of this *Roma aeterna,* whose head, the *caput mundi,* is the Capitol. This square was not regarded as an ordinary city square, but as the place from which the Romans formerly ruled the rest of the world. Michelangelo took into full account this conception of *Roma aeterna* when he was commissioned to rebuild the Capitol, which he boldly conceived as the *caput mundi.* The convex oval situated in the middle of the square appears to the viewer like the top of the globe; and the statue of Marcus Aurelius, placed in the center and at the highest point of this convex surface, is in the very axis of the sphere. The square is an organic unity, and the centrifugal forces—indicated by the starlike ornamentation drawn on the "sphere"—are opposed by the centripetal forces of the buildings which surround it.[33]

Michelangelo made the plans for the Capitol about 1546. In 1547 the task of rebuilding St. Peter's was assigned to him; he made it the symbol of the Kingdom of Christianity, a monument to the temporal and spiritual power of the Papacy. The immense dome pierces through the mass of the drum and hovers as if suspended and supported by its own strength, triumphing over matter—a true "heavenly" dome above the earth. It is the "crown" not only of St. Peter's but of the whole of Rome—of the world. Michelangelo goes back here to the old idea which saw in the dome the image of the heavenly vault.[34] But he does not show it in a merely static way. He expresses its birth as well: this dome, formed from matter, detaches itself from that matter and hovers majestically above it.[35]

In a similar way, Michelangelo's thoughts detached themselves from the temporal world to become concentrated more and more on the Kingdom which is not of this world and whose citizen he had become; his *Canzoniere spirituale* is proof of this. His political attitude dissolved into a religious one.

The way in which Michelangelo expressed political ideas by means of artistic forms differed from that of his contemporaries (Raphael, Salviati, Vasari, etc.), all of whom had directly glorified the political power which they served and had shown the triumphal effects of this power on contemporary life by means of historical tableaux. Michelangelo glorified neither political power nor the effects of this power on life, but symbolized its principles, i.e. the moral forces on which the political power of the Florentine Republic was based.[36] He separated the general from the particular and raised political thought to the level of ethics.

C H A P T E R

I I

Michelangelo's "Philosophy"

Iᴛ is almost impossible to separate precisely the different strands of Michelangelo's thought in any one work. It is difficult to say definitely whether a particular work expresses his philosophy or his religion or his political ideas, for they are often fused together. Still, one of these aspects does sometimes predominate, and it is the work of his mature years (from about 1510 to 1541) which best reveals the direction of his philosophical thought. Before this period, isolated tendencies toward a "philosophy" can be discerned in works having a religious, mythological, or political subject. Later his philosophical thought becomes assimilated with his religious thought. That is why this chapter finds its place between the one dealing with his political ideas and the one dealing with his religious opinions.

Michelangelo knew, at least through conversation, the philosophical doctrines of his time and he drew extensively from them. His contemporaries Berni, Vasari, Condivi, and

Varchi noticed that his poetry was "full of Platonic conceptions." [1] Several modern scholars have recognized the presence of Platonic and Neo-Platonic influences in his works of art as well. [2] To my mind, however, it has never been sufficiently emphasized that Michelangelo did not slavishly repeat these ideas but developed them in an original way, sometimes anticipating doctrines which philosophers and poets did not express until some generations later. This original development of Renaissance thought by Michelangelo is the subject of the present chapter.

Michelangelo never intended to develop a closed philosophical system. But at each stage in his life, he tried in different ways to define the philosophical attitude and to explain the meaning of existence. We shall examine here the progressive expansion of his thought, which began with man and ultimately embraced the universe. [3]

Among so many Renaissance minds affected by the ideas of Platonism, Michelangelo was perhaps the only one to find in such doctrines the metaphysical justification of his own personality. His own experiences corresponded to this philosophy. His experiences in love, first with Cavalieri, then with Vittoria Colonna, bore out Plato's theory that the worship of carnal beauty is merely a prelude to the contemplation of divine beauty. [4] The Platonic conception of the earthly life as not entirely real, as a life where the soul is held prisoner by matter, corroborated Michelangelo's profound dissatisfaction with the world and with himself. Hence his desire to free himself from this burden. [5] Plato's belief that the intellect is capable, in its moments of exaltation, of glimpsing through earthly forms the divine light which it knew before descending to earth, which it is always longing to see again, and toward which it can rise again, "della carne ancor vestita," still clothed in flesh—this belief confirmed Michelangelo's experience.

Varchi, a contemporary and friend of the artist, wrote in his commentary on one of Michelangelo's sonnets: "The greatest power that can be bestowed upon man is the faculty of soaring to the heavens, while still belonging to earth, and of becoming not just an angel but God himself." We can, still in our earthly bodies, rise to the heavens, and be transformed from men into God. This is the doctrine of deification.[6]

These Platonic and Neo-Platonic doctrines were circulated thanks to the Latin translations, by Marsilio Ficino, of Plato's dialogues and the works of the Neo-Platonists (Plotinus, Jamblicus, Proclus).[7] Ficino also wrote commentaries on the works he translated. His commentary on the *Symposium* became the classic work on the conception of love during the Renaissance, and was the model for numerous dialogues and treatises on love written during this period.

Michelangelo had a poor knowledge of Latin (in Giannotti's dialogue he complains—he was then seventy years old —of not having learned that classical language well). Perhaps he could not read these translations; but in all probability he knew Plato's doctrines from his personal acquaintance with the members of the Platonic Academy—Marsilio Ficino, Benivieni, Pico della Mirandola, and Poliziano—when he lived during his youth as a guest in the palace of Lorenzo de' Medici. He certainly knew the poems of his patron Lorenzo de' Medici, and probably Pico della Mirandola's Italian commentary on the *Canzone d'Amore* by Benivieni. The study of Dante and Petrarch would have deepened his interest in Plato's doctrines. He must have been familiar with Landino's famous commentary interpreting the *Divina Commedia* in a Neo-Platonic sense. Michelangelo had assimilated these Platonic ideas so completely that he could control them at will, and far from slavishly illustrating them in his art, he freely philosophized with his brush, his chisel, and his pen. It may be said that he handled the essential ideas of Platonism in a new way, and that instead of merely reproducing a philosophical system already established by a theologian or a philosopher, he created works of original thought.

A clear understanding of divine things is made possible, according to the young Michelangelo, only through a seizure of the soul, the *furor divinus*. The spirit of God then takes complete possession of the body, elevating the soul and the spirit to a knowledge of the supernatural. This is not merely an ecstasy of *feeling*, such as was later conceived by the Baroque, but an ecstasy of *spirit*. The books and scrolls which Michelangelo puts into the hands of his seers show clearly that he is dealing with the elevation of the spirit. His saints, apostles, prophets, and sibyls are in the grip of metaphysical forces. They are detached from the material world of the *hic et nunc* and are bound to the Absolute, to Truth, to God. This is how Michelangelo understands our knowledge of divine things; this is his conception of the true philosopher.

Only the Virgin is shown in a state of contemplation, without the intermediary of the *furor divinus*. She is endowed with the faculty of recognizing the supernatural through the calm meditation of her spirit.

Seated on a square stone block, and quite without adornment, the *Virgin of the Steps* seems to be absorbed in her thoughts and to care nothing for the world around her. She is the Genetrix, carrying life itself in her womb, but she is also a sibyl, whose glance seems to read the future and to glimpse the tragic end of the Child born to her. We are far from the smiling, worldly Virgins of the Florentine Quattrocento. This Virgin is Michelangelo's vision of the Primordial Mother, at once the source of life and the bearer of death. She is a sibyl whose mind ponders the essence of things, and indeed destiny itself.[8]

The *Virgin of Bruges*, to take another example, no longer gracefully inclines her head in the manner of Quattrocento

(34)

Virgins. Severe and frontal, she has a hieratic aspect. The Child, instead of being seated on her lap, is standing between her knees. He seems to be about to break away from his mother and climb down toward life. The anxiety lurking behind the apparent impassivity of the mother is betrayed in the slight contraction of her eyebrows and the almost imperceptible pouting of her lips. Again we are in the presence of a prescient Virgin.[9]

In this way the sibylline Virgins of Michelangelo's youth reveal his conception of *contemplatio:* it is the act of meditation, made possible by a certain quality of spirit, upon destiny itself.[10]

The philosophy of history and the philosophy of nature did not play a large role in the thought of the master at this stage of his career; he looked at existence *sub specie aeternitatis* and focused his attention rather on what is immutable than on what is subject to change.

The *Doni Virgin* is the epitome of Michelangelo's "philosophy of history." Even stylistically she is different from the master's other Virgins of the same period. This Virgin is a bare-armed, muscular heroine, holding the Child aloft on her shoulder with the gesture of an amphora bearer. And to the difference in form corresponds a difference in content. The idea of placing one figure on another's shoulder traditionally symbolizes the victory of a new principle over an old one; the masters of the Middle Ages sometimes placed the Apostles on the shoulders of the Prophets in this way. The Virgin and St. Joseph both belong by birth to the world of the Old Testament *sub lege;* but the Child, watched ecstatically by the Virgin, whose glance is full of hope and adoration, represents the future world of the New Testament *sub gratia.* He is no longer an innocent child but a young savior hero, his head

(35)

PLATE V

bound by the ribbon of the victorious athlete. He is looking at his mother gravely, as if conscious of his mission.

In the background, separated by a low wall, are two groups of supple, curly-headed ephebes. They seem to be either seated upon or leaning against an unfinished tribune, like those in ancient thermae. This may be intended as a pagan building which would be finished as a Christian apse. One of the ephebes is embracing his friend. A third seems to be jealous of this display. To the left, two more youths are dreamily watching the love scene. These groups probably represent the pagan world, which does not understand the nobler bonds of love uniting the Holy Family.[11] Only the little St. John, among those behind the wall, is watching the sacred scene with ecstatic admiration. He represents the link between the two worlds.[12]

The group in the foreground is as if carved from a single cylindrical block seen inside a transparent sphere—the globe of the earth, filled with the three epochs of humanity. Such a "philosophy of history" belongs to the tradition of the Middle Ages, but the way in which Michelangelo expresses it is personal. For him the ancient pagan world is superior in beauty to the Christian one, and the one stems from the other.

In his early works, Michelangelo's "philosophy of nature" also appears to keep within the limits of tradition. His *Bacchus* seems to personify the cosmic cycle of birth, decline, death, and rebirth. Boccaccio (in his *De Genealogia Deorum*) describes Bacchus as a personification of the cosmic forces. This work may have inspired Michelangelo when he created his statue, which bears so little resemblance to any other Bacchus of the Renaissance. Here too the composition develops in a spiral, marked by the three heads: the tiger's mask (in this case actually a lion's mask), the head of the joyous little satyr, and the face of Bacchus. The little satyr incarnates the forces of rebirth; Bacchus, with his heavy head, his body

(36)

PLATE VII

swollen with sap, and his reeling posture, signifies degener-
ation. The mask is the symbol of death. The three heads form
a cyclical movement.[13]

Thus it is possible to deduce from Michelangelo's early
works what he considered man's philosophical attitude to be,
and even to see in them the rudiments of a philosophy of history and a philosophy of nature. But it is only in the three
great works of his maturity—the Tomb of Julius II, the Ceiling
of the Sistine Chapel, and the Medici Chapel—that we can
grasp what he considered the "system of the world" to be.

According to the orders of Julius II, a true Renaissance
man haunted by imperial dreams, the tomb was to exalt his
martial power and triumphs. It was to be, says Vasari, a
monument to the glorification of the Supreme Pontiff, all-
victorious and all-conquering.

When Michelangelo made his first sketches, his ambition
no doubt was to fashion a monument which would satisfy the
demands of the Pope. But in the course of the work, the
triumphal mausoleum prescribed by Julius II was transformed
into a monument which revealed the progressive states of catharsis of the human soul. This new meaning became more
and more clear, in spite of the monument's reduction in size,
determined by external circumstances, and forced Michelangelo to revise the architecture and the symbolic figures six
times. Finally he reached the point of partially rejecting even
the statues which had already been executed (a *Victory* and
the *Slaves*) in order to obey his inner voice.[14]

The first project, dated 1505, of which only two contemporary descriptions remain,[15] was for a free-standing mausoleum consisting of three superimposed zones. The bottom
zone was conceived as the "house of the dead," with an oval
cella inside; in the lateral niches, Victories, a kinds of guard,
were to be placed. In front of the pilasters framing these
niches, there were to be Slaves, meant as trophies and

(37)

PLATE XXVIII

mounted on rectangular bases.[16] In the second zone, above the niches, colossal seated figures of Moses and St. Paul, and allegories of the Active and the Contemplative Life, were to be set on a platform. And in the third zone, on an oval base, would rest the sarcophagus, with the reclining figure of the Pope flanked by allegories of Heaven and Earth.[17]

Michelangelo kept the same structure of three superimposed zones in the second project, dated 1513 (whose preparatory drawing is preserved in Berlin),[18] but enlarged the top zone by the addition of a monumental niche, called the "capelletta" in the documents, which was to enframe the Virgin and Child above the papal sarcophagus. The top of the triumphal monument was now Christianized. By adding this new element he completely changed the general effect: instead of a graded pyramid, there now rose a dynamic composition in two superimposed and contrasted spheres; the squat, massive bottom zone now served only as a base for the large seated figures; in the middle, like a vision, a dreamlike architecture suddenly soared with mounting tension.

The bottom zone symbolizes the earthly existence of the human soul, with its alternating victories and defeats. Defeat is incarnate in the Slaves. These are adolescents with supple, athletic bodies, bearing no resemblance to the slaves represented in earlier triumphal monuments. In antiquity and in the Renaissance before Michelangelo, slaves always belonged to alien races (barbarian or Negro). Michelangelo made them heroic and as beautiful as possible; sometimes resigned, sometimes in revolt against their fate, they are not personifications of provinces subjugated by the Pope (as Vasari would have it) or of the mourning liberal arts (Condivi) but symbols of the human soul imprisoned in the body. Michelangelo certainly was acquainted with this metaphor. We know this from a page in the Buonarroti Archives in Florence on which he wrote in his own hand the following phrase from Petrarch's

(38)

Triumph of Death: "La morte è 'l fin d'una prigione scura." Death is the end of a dark prison, i.e. Life is the dark prison of the soul.[19]

The middle zone symbolizes the supraterrestrial existence of the soul and the intellect. Moses and St. Paul were considered in the Bible and by Renaissance Neo-Platonists to be counterparts, for both arrived through a synthesis of the active life and the contemplative life at a vision of the "face of God"—as Pico della Mirandola points out in his commentary on Benivieni's *Canzone d'Amore.*[20]

In the top zone, the soul, freed from its body, appears in its celestial life. This is the apotheosis, that is, the spiritual triumph of the Pope.

One can see why Michelangelo transformed his first project, and deliberately contrasted the celestial sphere with the terrestrial one. In this way the work, seen as a whole, shows the stages of the soul's gradual purification and ascension from the earthly to the heavenly life. But the symbols of the "states of the soul" are at the same time the building blocks of the objective edifice of the universe. This is because Michelangelo seems, like Dante, to have assumed a perfect parallelism between the inner life of the soul and the outer hierarchic structure of the world.

Seen as a hierarchic image of the world, the bottom zone is the world *ante legem,* conceived according to the pagan symbolism of the Trionfi and presented in a style which is antique in feeling. The intermediary zone is the world *sub lege* conceived in a "protobaroque" style. The top zone is the world *sub gratia,* where Michelangelo is inspired by the verticalism of the Gothic style. The historical periods are no longer successive, but have become the simultaneous stages of the hierarchy of the structure of the universe. The originality of the Tomb of Julius II, compared with earlier Italian tombs, lies precisely in this hierarchy of three stages.[21] For the first time a tomb is not only the house of the dead but a sort of diagram of the system of the world.

This is not the place for a detailed analysis of the Sistine Ceiling. What I shall try to do is to bring out the dominating thought of this work, and then give some striking examples of the Platonic influences in its details.[22]

The painted architectural framework forms a kind of immense trellis which soars before our eyes, and through whose bars our glance plunges into an ideal world. The historical frescoes (*storie*) above us present another reality, governed by its own laws and superimposing an ideal world, a sort of Olympus, upon our own world.

Michelangelo's monumental framework divides the Ceiling into three zones, one above the other, and to these topographically and stylistically separate zones corresponds a triple hierarchy of content which is reminiscent of the Tomb of Julius II. The bottom zone, consisting of lunettes and concave triangles (*vele*), is peopled by a race enduring the eternal vicissitudes of the human condition. In the second zone above, the large figures of the Prophets and Sibyls are seated on thrones. Although they are human, they rise above their condition through their gift of clairvoyance. They know how to extract from life its divine element and are able to interpret the mind of the Eternal. Lastly, the third zone, which seems to be at once framed by and behind the monumental architectural skeleton, contains both the history of man in his direct relationship with the divine, and the history of God Himself.

The universe is conceived therefore as an "architectural structure" consisting of three degrees or superimposed levels. This is a pagan idea which had survived the Middle Ages.[23]

Michelangelo did not have complete freedom in his choice

(40)

PLATE XXX

of subject, or in the order of the frescoes. A quarter of a century before, the masters of the Quattrocento had already decorated the walls of the chapel with two cycles, relating the story of Moses on the left wall and the story of Jesus Christ on the right. They had represented these subjects as corresponding typologically and as retracing the history of humanity *sub lege* and *sub gratia*. When Michelangelo decided that he too would paint historical scenes, there remained only one subject he could use to complete the two preceding ones, that is, the story of humanity *ante legem*. Furthermore, as the Quattrocento artists had unfolded their cycles from the altar toward the entrance—according to the traditions of early Christian art (the ancient basilicas of St. Peter and St. Paul), Michelangelo was limited by this as well. He was obliged to begin his cycle at the back of the chapel, and to finish it above the entrance door.

But on the biblical meaning of his work Michelangelo seems to have imposed a new significance, a Platonic interpretation of Genesis.[24] Because of a philosophic conception of human existence, drawn not from the teaching of the Church but from Platonism and the Neo-Platonism of the Renaissance, he added depth to the original iconographic program.

The viewer who advances from the main entrance toward the altar experiences as he passes from history to history a feeling of gradual ascension. This impression of successive liberation is deliberately accentuated by the use of three different compositional patterns. In the first three frescoes the fields, in the manner of ancient reliefs, are filled with numerous relatively small figures; in the next three the histories are composed of a few large-sized figures all in the foreground, which repeat in their respective positions the general tension of the ceiling; finally, in the last three frescoes the movements of the figures of God the Father are independent of the form of the ceiling and of the architectural framework, so that these compositions seem to offer a glimpse of the infinite. By identifying himself with the sublime movement of the Supreme Being, the viewer himself feels the chains of this earthly life fall away and is raised into the sphere of absolute liberty. The divine origin of the human soul becomes manifest. This theme of the ascension from the prison of the body to the freedom inherent in the soul is a favorite of the Platonic literature of the Renaissance (Ficino, Lorenzo de' Medici, Landino, Pico, Castiglione). The idea is expressed in several of Michelangelo's poems:

> 'l mezzo di me, che dal ciel viene,
> A quel con gran desir ritorna e vola . . .
> (Frey, *Dicht.* CIX, 66–70)

(That half of me which comes from heaven
turns back towards it with a great longing,
and flies . . .)

> L'anima, della carne ancor vestita,
> Con esso è già più volte asciesa a Dio.
> (Frey, *Dicht.* LXIV)

(The soul, still clothed in flesh, has even so
ascended several times to God.)

The motif of the winged soul, as it is found in the *Phaedrus,* inspired the following verses:

> Amore isveglia e desta e'mpenna l'ale
> Nè l'alto vol prescrive al van furore,
> Qual primo grado, c'al suo creatore,
> Di quel non sazia, l'alma ascende e sale.
> (Frey, *Dicht.* XCI)

(Love awakens and gives wings to the soul
when it reaches the first level; not satiated
by this, it ascends and rises to its creator.)

The ideas of emanation and re-emanation are united in the passage where Michelangelo speaks of Dante:

Dal ciel discese, e col mortal suo, poi
Che visto ebbe l'inferno giusto e'l pio,
Ritornò vivo a contemplare Dio . . .

(Frey, Dicht. CIX, 37)

(He came down from heaven; and when in his mortal body, he had seen the hell of justice and of mercy, he went back, living, to contemplate God.)

C'altro non è c'al mondo mi dilecti:
Ascender vivo fra gli spiriti eletti . . .

(Frey, Dicht. CXLI)

(Nothing in this world gives me pleasure but to ascend, still living, among the spirits of the elect.)

These verses offer a striking analogy to the central idea of the Sistine Ceiling.

The whole series of frescoes shows, then, the return to God of the human soul imprisoned in the body—that is, the idea of *deificatio* or *ritorno a Dio*. The soul can free itself from the bonds of the flesh only by returning to God. This return to God is but the return of the soul to its own source and true essence, for to the Platonists of the Renaissance, God is simply the Idea of man, and not a transcendent being as was taught traditionally. Pico della Mirandola formulated the theory in his *Heptaplus*. Michelangelo's last five frescoes above the presbyterium show, together with the gradual metamorphosis of the figure of God, the progressive deification of man, that is to say, the realization of his highest innate faculties.

The vision of the divine being changes here from an anthropomorphic to a uranian form (the form of a cloud, bird,

(43)

PLATES XXX, XXXII

and planet). These visions also reveal the development of the divine intelligence from limited ideas (*The Creation of Eve*) to omniscience (*The Creation of Adam*). Not being constrained by space, time, and matter, the creative force freely develops its own being. This is "the development of the supreme being, which is determined by nothing and which determines everything" (Landino). Finally, in the last fresco the cosmic force dominates like a hurricane in the midst of primeval chaos.

Perhaps Michelangelo was inspired, in his idea of superimposing the significance of the *ascensio* or *ritorno a Dio* on the biblical scenes of Genesis, by the fact that the Sistine Chapel was consecrated to the Assumption. The original ceiling decoration by P. M. d'Amelia represented a sky dotted with golden stars. According to the aesthetic principles of the Cinquecento, an organic correspondence had to be established between the significance and purpose of a given space and the decoration of that space (Armenini, A. Caro). It was therefore logical, in Michelangelo's view, to paint, in a chapel dedicated to the Assumption, frescoes representing the progressive elevation of the soul. In addition, the insertion of this content of *deificatio* into biblical scenes allowed Michelangelo to offer to the viewer a visual and spiritual unity progressing in the direction of the altar, despite the fact that chronologically the biblical cycle unfolded from the altar toward the entrance. Platonic interpretations of Genesis were in any case not unknown to the period, and some go back to the twelfth century. The most celebrated Renaissance example was Pico's *Heptaplus*. This book did not serve as a direct source for Michelangelo, but a similar method of interpretation can be found in it.

It is not just the cycle as a whole which expresses an idea dear to the philosophy of the time (the *ascensio* and the *deificatio* of the soul); the details of the frescoes themselves

(44)

PLATE XXXI

abound in visual symbols taken from Neo-Platonism. According to the Platonists, for instance, the body was the dungeon of the soul, and the Renaissance philosophers symbolized this captivity by drunkenness (Landino). Michelangelo's drunken Noah, placed like the statue of an ancient river god on a wooden base, with his powerful and muscular body, seems nevertheless to be the prisoner of that body. In other words, to regard drunkenness as a fetter of the body was a concept perfectly in accordance with Platonic doctrines.

Another Platonic belief was that "Divine wisdom creates all things visible and invisible in the image of the *idea* in the divine mind" (Zuccari). So, in the *Creation of Eve,* God the Father evokes in matter the conception in his mind. Indeed, Michelangelo's God the Father conceives new beings by thought (*idea*) alone, by a gesture of conjuration, and not by the material act of drawing Eve from Adam's side, as his predecessors had done. The next history—the *Creation of Adam*—illustrates the divine omniscience. God is represented in the uranian form of an anthropomorphic cloud, surrounded by genii. Besides the eight genii, who symbolize perhaps the eight celestial spheres, there are two other genii, set apart from the rest and of different aspect, under the arm of God. One has a girl's face and is watching Adam with an intense and fascinated gaze; the other is a child, with the same posture and features as the Jesus Christs done by Michelangelo before this. It is possible, as J. P. Richter suggested more than a century ago, that the young woman represents "Eve not yet created," that is to say the Platonic Idea of Eve, preexisting in the divine intellect; the child would be Jesus Christ, also pre-existing in God's mind. These two figures reveal that divine omniscience in which the entire history of humanity is contained simultaneously.[25]

In the *Separation of Light from Darkness*, the last history of the cycle, God seems to be emerging from chaos. Here

(45)

PLATES XXXI, XXXII

Michelangelo went beyond an iconographic tradition already more than a thousand years old. The body of God the Father seems to be the condensation of a cloudy substance, soft and almost ethereal. God appears to be formed of the substance of the clouds, from which at the same time he is trying to disengage himself. This is an idea that comes directly or indirectly from the ancient cosmogonies; according to these, in the beginning only matter (*hyle*) existed, which subsequently condensed itself in the form of the heavenly bodies. Again, in its dynamism, this vision anticipates the modern conception of the origin of the universe as described by Laplace.[26]

Finally, the Prophets and Sibyls complete the composition. It is their visions which appear in the histories of the central axis. These supernatural beings, endowed with strength of body and superiority of spirit, illuminated by their *spiritualis ignis*, are always accompanied by two little genii. By iconographic tradition these were angels of inspiration—indeed in the early preparatory sketches Michelangelo represented them as winged angels. But the master now gives them the aspect of pagan genii, naked and wingless. The Neo-Platonists of the Renaissance identified Christian angels with daemons and pagan genii. They said in the manner of Plato that every man is accompanied by two daemons or genii: these are the two opposing souls which dwell within us, the spiritual and the sensual (Varchi). These genii become the two tendencies of the intellect of the Prophets and Sibyls in Michelangelo as well. They are no longer messengers who transmit the will of God (Giovanni Pisano), but projections of the intellectual being of the Prophets and Sibyls, projections which follow the inner movements of their spirit.

This is not all: above and below the Prophets and Sibyls are placed other figures—nudes—which can also be explained in terms of Neo-Platonism, according to which the microcosm of man consists of three stages, or *gradi: natura corporale,*

PLATE X

the body; *anima razionale,* the soul; *natura intellettuale* or *intellettiva,* the intellect. Each of these stages possesses its own life principle; it seems that Michelangelo personified these stages in his three different kinds of nude genii. We have already seen how he embodied the *natura intellettuale* in the little genii who are behind and beside the Prophets and Sibyls. So it would be natural to suppose that he embodied the *natura corporale* in the *putti* below these figures, and that he transformed the *anima razionale* into the genii above their heads, the magnificent Ignudi. Consequently each Prophet and each Sibyl is accompanied by the "spirits" which constitute his triple nature; each one, surrounded by his satellites, forms a sort of solar system.[27]

So it is that some of the most important philosophic and religious beliefs of the Renaissance are fused in the Sistine Ceiling: the fundamental idea is the conception of earthly beauty as a divine manifestation; the belief in the possibility of a *renovatio* of the human soul, whose nature is divine (Prophets and Sibyls), linked to the idea of the *ascensio* and the *deificatio* of the soul. The Sistine Ceiling represents the *summa* of the ideals of Renaissance man, a compendium of the artistic, philosophic, and religious trends of the era, a veritable *Divina Commedia* of the Renaissance.

And yet, the Ceiling is not just a review of Florentine Neo-Platonism; it is an original development of its ideas. For although the principles of spiritual ascension and deification were known to the philosophy of the Renaissance, Michelangelo was the first to articulate them. In his work the Supreme Being goes through an evolution for the first time. In Renaissance philosophy the Absolute Being is changeless and immobile. Change is for the Neo-Platonists a sign of submission to time; the Supreme Being is considered as substance. Michelangelo on the contrary considers the Supreme Being as a force, and in his work evolution seems to be determined by the divine immanent will. God is more powerful when He creates greater works. His creative force determines not only the work but His own form. God is no longer conceived exclusively as a substance but as a function as well; He is the creative force, the "absolute artist." The concept of God as a creative force is found in Nicholas of Cusa also, but only in the form of passing references.[28] Michelangelo was the first to give it concrete form.

The Medici Chapel is the third great work by Michelangelo in which he employs and handles with ease the substance of Platonism. The composition of the tombs seen as a whole represented in the first versions the apotheosis of the *Duchi*, their victory over the dark forces of existence; the final version shows the liberation of the soul after death from the *carcer terreno*, the body. The allegories of Time—Dawn and Dusk, Day and Night—and of the rivers of Hades (which in the original project were to be placed below those of Time) symbolize those inexorable forces of destiny which rule the life of mortal man. These athletic figures weigh upon the perishable bodies enclosed in the sarcophagi and dominate them, while the immortal souls of the dead free themselves from the coffins, whose lids appear to be cleft in the middle, and rise above them into a region inaccessible to the blind forces of time. Freed from the shackles of the body, the souls (of the *Duchi*) find themselves again in their true essence, through eternal contemplation of the idea of life, symbolized by the Virgin suckling her Child. The two *Duchi* are turned toward the Virgin and are contemplating her.

This *Medici Virgin* is placed so that she faces the altar and is the key to the chapel's composition. She is seated on a high, narrow block, with only one foot touching the ground, and this confers on her being a mysterious levitation. The slender, powerful proportions of her body show through her diaphanous garments. The muscular child, seated astride her knee,

(48)

PLATES XXXIII, XXXIV, XV

is turning toward her in a violent movement and clutching avidly at her breast. His back is to the viewer. The sap of life flowing into him seems to swell him with new strength. The mother is all abnegation; she offers her body to the child, bracing herself on her right arm. Her head is inclined, her face with its serious features is marked by a pensive expression of tenderness. Mother and son seem to be one single being, strikingly epitomizing the cyclic idea of life: eternal attrition and eternal renewal.

Thus a chapel consecrated to death becomes the sanctuary of what is called the true life of the soul. It is an organic unity, a complete world—the receptacle of the souls of the departed.

The resemblance is evident between the fundamental ideas expressed here and those of Plato on death and the immortality of the soul. In the *Phaedo* Plato describes the life of the soul beyond the grave. The soul, freed from its corporeal prison, returns to that world which it has always desired and which is its real home. There, at last it can devote itself to the contemplation of ideas in the same way that Michelangelo's Medici dukes are contemplating the Virgin.[29] To demonstrate the rebirth of the soul after the death of the body, Plato uses, among others, an argument based on a natural law, which he calls "the generation of opposing principles." According to this law, given two opposing principles there must necessarily exist two "opposing methods of generation." Plato then cites as example the state of wakefulness which follows the state of sleep, whose methods of generation are waking and somnolence. This explains—as Oeri has already noted—why in the allegories Michelangelo did not represent the four states of the soul in their natural succession, and why he grouped them in opposite pairs.[30] Further, we find in the *Phaedo* the four rivers of Hades symbolizing eternal fluctuation, just as Michelangelo meant to express it in his original project.

In view of the fact that this chapel was consecrated to the Resurrection of Christ, the prototype of all resurrection, the use here of the basic theme of the *Phaedo* should not be regarded as surprising. The Neo-Platonic philosophy of the Renaissance saw in the Platonic doctrine of the rebirth of the human soul after death a prophecy of the Christian doctrine of the Resurrection. Ficino, in his commentary on the *Phaedo*, says: "Sicut ex viventibus fiunt mortui, sic ex mortuis viventes, quandoque resurgere. Ubi videtur mortuorum resurrectionem vaticinari." The two doctrines having been linked together by Ficino, it was but a step further to portray the Platonic doctrine of the soul's rebirth in a chapel dedicated to the Christian Resurrection.

So it is clear that the origin of the composition of the Medici Chapel derives from Plato's myths, especially his *Phaedo*. But only Michelangelo knew how to weld the elements of these myths into an organic whole, and insert them into an architectural structure. Using Plato's scattered and somewhat vague elements, he created a firmly constructed world, which lays bare the secret workings of death and of the soul's life after death.

Michelangelo's *Last Judgment* (1536–41), executed after the Medici Chapel, is above all else an eschatological vision. The peaceful kingdom of heaven depicted in traditional works gives way to a stormy sky. A whirlwind tosses the cyclopean bodies like so many toys. Anguish dominates the scene: anguish before judgment and before the judge, who is here a fulminating Jupiter.[31]

But Michelangelo did not confine himself to portraying human terror in the face of annihilation. He superimposed a cosmological meaning on the eschatological meaning. He revealed the laws of attraction and of the movement of bodies in cosmic space. This aspect of the work may be regarded as philosophical. It is a grandiose vision of a heliocentric uni-

(50)

PLATE XXXV

verse. Christ is the center of a solar system around which gravitate all the constellations in a circular movement. It is not by chance that this beardless, youthful Christ, with his flowing hair and perfect body, is so like an Apollo. Antiquity had endowed the god, whose personality it had identified with that of Helios, with the two opposing powers of the sun: the powers of nourishing and destroying. Again, Christianity had from the beginning identified Christ with the sun, and had transferred to him the characteristics of Helios: out of the *Sol Invictus* it fashioned the *Sol Justitiae*.[32] So Michelangelo found the idea of identifying Christ with Apollo already in existence. By reserving a central role for the Sun-Christ, whose magic power commands the unity of the macrocosm, the artist succeeded in his own way in creating a religious vision of the universe, which curiously anticipates that of his contemporary Copernicus. The idea behind Michelangelo's composition is seven years earlier than the publication of Copernicus' discovery in 1543. What happened was that both of them revived the heliocentric hypothesis already formulated by antiquity.

The medieval symbol of Fortune is a woman with a wheel in her hand. This wheel ensnares men and drags them on, by turns raising them up and casting them into the abyss: man is an instrument of the forces of nature. He does not pit himself directly against these forces. During the early Renaissance another symbol was substituted for this one. Fortuna is now a woman controlling by hand the sail of a boat with man at the helm, a symbol of the new conception of man trusting in his own strength; he is no longer dominated by Fortuna but dominates her. Here is the optimism of the Renaissance before Savonarola, which finds expression in this sentence by L. B. Alberti (*Della tranquillità dell' animo.* Lib. III, *Op. Volgari* I, 113 f.): "La fortuna per sè, non dubitare, sempre fu e sempre sarà inbecillissima et debolissima, a chi se gli opponga." (Fortune in itself, without any doubt, has always been and always will be very stupid and weak toward those who oppose it.) [33]

In the circular movements which flow through the *Last Judgment*, Michelangelo returns to the earlier conception of Fortune (the wheel). But man is no longer a passive instrument. He is a titan in revolt against the forces of destiny which, in spite of his efforts to free himself, hold him in thrall. It is evident that in this standard philosophic problem of the Renaissance, the problem of the relationship between *freedom* and *fate*, Michelangelo goes beyond the Renaissance idea of liberty and arrives finally at a cosmic conception of fate. Belief in the power of man is visible in his work; but at the same time man is subjugated by the forces of the universe. The optimism of the early Renaissance has been transcended. Rotation, considered as a fundamental law which plays upon the movements of bodies in the space of the macrocosm, was also to decide the composition of the master's last two frescoes: those in the Pauline Chapel. [34]

The center of Michelangelo's philosophical interest had now been transferred from man to the universe. Where the subject of the Tomb of Julius II and of the Sistine Ceiling had been man (the soul) and his *deificatio*, springing from the titanism of the artist's youth and early maturity, the subject of the *Last Judgment* and the Pauline frescoes was the revelation of the cosmic forces by which man is bound.

This progression corresponded to the general development of human thought during the Renaissance. [35] Under the influence of its discoveries, particularly those of Copernicus, man's conception of the universe was completely transformed during this era. In enlightened circles at least, a cosmocentric point of view replaced the anthropocentric view. This idea found its most perfect expression in philosophy and literature only at the end of the century, in the works of Giordano Bruno and Jacob Boehme. It is worth noting that Michelangelo pre-

(52)

PLATES XXXVI, XXXVII

ceded them, and that the inner logic of his development led him in this same direction. In the Sistine Ceiling man was still the summit of creation, and the whole work was a crowning point of Renaissance humanism. In the Medici Chapel, this anthropocentric ideal was transformed and Michelangelo offered a glimpse of the blind forces of nature (allegories) to which man is subject and from which only the soul can escape. In the *Last Judgment,* he finally achieved a macrocosmic system, where titanic man is a nothing in the face of destiny; and here we admire a grandiose anticipation of the systems of the universe envisioned by Bruno, Campanella, Boehme.[36]

Another manifestation of humanist ideals is to be found in the "philosophy of love" expressed in Michelangelo's poetry, particularly in the poems dedicated to Tommaso Cavalieri and Vittoria Colonna. This is a completely Platonic philosophy in which the ideas of the *raptus* of the soul, of the *ascensio* and *deificatio,* can be recognized, ideas already implicit in the Sistine Ceiling, but now, from about 1532 to 1547, refined, spiritualized, and divested of youthful titanism. The *deificatio* is accomplished no longer through solitary contemplation, but on the contrary by fusion of the soul with that of the beloved.

Because this philosophy of love is so closely bound to the concept of beauty—for it is beauty, according to Michelangelo and the Platonists, that gives birth to love—the whole problem will be examined in the last chapter, which deals with Michelangelo's artistic credo.

The thought of death haunted Michelangelo from his earliest youth. He believed himself to be among those whose natures belong to the night. On February 22, 1555, he wrote to Vasari: "No thought forms in me, but that death is sculptured there." Death in his view was not to be separated from life. Death was an integral part of life. He once said: "If life pleases us, death, being made by the hands of the same creator, should not displease us." [37] Death does not come from without; it is inherent in existence from birth. To this conception of death can be attributed the stoical attitude toward death expressed so often in the Virgins of his youth. But, in this early period, Michelangelo was not yet preoccupied by the life beyond the grave. His philosophy of death reached a new stage when he spiritualized his conception of the soul (under the influence of Platonism), and recognized the dualism which exists between the life of the soul in the body and the life of the soul beyond the grave. Now the earthly life was for him a struggle against matter, and death was deliverance. This is what he expressed in the Tomb of Julius II. There life beyond the grave was still fairly vague and abstract. But finally, in the Medici Chapel, this life beyond the grave acquired an explicit content, that is, the spiritual contemplation of the *idea* by the souls of the departed.

As a consequence of his religious conversion toward the end of his life, Michelangelo went beyond Platonic dualism. Death now became a dissolution of solitary existence, and brought about the integration of the individual soul with divine love, into whose being it dissolved (Pietàs in Florence and Milan). This is perhaps the reason for the strange emanation of tenderness from the roughly indicated forms and broken lines.

So far only the metaphysical and cosmological elements in the art and thought of Michelangelo have been mentioned. A word must now be said about the practical philosophy, or

PLATES I, III, IV, XXVIII, XXIX, XXXIII, XXVII

rather the wisdom, of the artist, a wisdom which guided him throughout his life. He loved the solitary life, says Vasari, as do all those enamoured of art which demands man's whole being.

In Donato Giannotti's *Dialogue,* Michelangelo sums up his wisdom in this way: "If a man wishes to find himself and to enjoy his individuality he must not give himself up to joys and pleasures, but must think of death. This is the only thought which will teach him to know himself, which will keep him concentrated within himself, without dissipating himself and allowing relatives, friends, masters, ambitions, avarice, and other sins to steal from him what they can steal from a man. The effect of this thought on death is marvelous, for just as it destroys everything else, it preserves and maintains those who think of it and protects them against all human passions." [38]

Michelangelo's philosophical works are not simply a translation, in painting or sculpture, of a given philosophy; in themselves they represent, by means of visual symbols, a creative synthesis of transcendent idealism. This synthesis is clearer and more coherent than that found in the works of the philosophers and poets of the Platonic Academy of the late Quattrocento. Landino, Ficino, and Pico were incapable of expressing their ideas in an orderly way. The conclusion might be drawn that the fine arts constituted the principal means for the expression of a world view in the Renaissance.

CHAPTER

III

Michelangelo's Religious Outlook

I n order to penetrate more deeply into Michelangelo's inner life and thus complete our study of his political beliefs and philosophical conceptions, an elucidation of the master's religious thought is necessary.

This chapter will focus on the form and development of his religious attitudes, and seek to explain the influence of these attitudes, and of the new religious doctrines, on the iconography and style of his works.[1]

Let us consider Michelangelo's reaction to the religious trends of his time. The great contemporary religious thinkers made a vivid impression on him—in his youth he was fascinated by the sermons of Savonarola, and in his old age by the ideas emanating from the "Italian Catholic Reform" of Juan de Valdés and his circle. Nevertheless he remained faithful to the traditions of the Church. So two different aspects of his religious life can be observed: on the one hand traditional Catholicism; on the other the ideas of the reformers Savonarola and Valdés. Michelangelo does not appear to have been conscious of this duality, and the two tendencies seem to have coexisted without contradicting each other in his mind. His traditional piety is revealed in his letters to his family; the new ideas find expression in his works of art and his poetry.

Evidence of the traditional side of Michelangelo's religion is scattered throughout his whole life. He was a practicing Catholic. He believed in the efficacy of prayer and made it a habit to have prayers said for the success of his works before he finished them.[2] For example, in 1507, before he finished the bronze statue of Julius II in Bologna, he requested that prayers be said in Florence (Milanesi, pp. 76 and 88). In 1511 and 1512, before completing the Sistine Ceiling, he made the same request. He also believed in the efficacy of the Sacraments. During his father's serious illness in 1516, he asked his brother Buonarroto to see to it that the former received the "last rites of the Church." On the death of his brother Giovansimone, he inquired anxiously (1548, Milanesi, p. 217) "se è morto confessato e communicato con tutte le cose ordinate dalla Chiesa" (if he died shriven and if he had received communion according to the rites of the Church). When he learned that Giovansimone had not received communion, but that he had repented, he declared himself satisfied and wrote (1548, Milanesi, p. 219) "e questa per la salute basta" (that will be enough for his salvation). He believed in the efficacy of good works, almsgiving, and charity. In a series of letters dated 1547, 1548, 1549, 1550, 1551, and 1561 he asked his nephew to give alms for the salvation of his soul, and also for the soul of his brother Buonarroto.[3]

This formalistic traditional piety never left him, and toward the end of his life Michelangelo became more and more devout; but his personal, antiformalistic religious attitudes evolved according to the different periods of his life. In those times of passionate dispute over dogma, reaching a point where the true faith was often lost sight of, Michelangelo sought after a personal belief.

Generally speaking, a work of art's subject matter is not essential to its religious character. The religious spirit really comes out in a work if that work has sprung from a broader conception of man, no longer viewed as a self-sufficient microcosm but as a being determined by powers superior and exterior to him. From the very beginning, man is not autonomous in Michelangelo's works, but is governed by superhuman powers. The artist gives concrete expression to a religious belief—but it is not yet a specifically Christian belief, for the unseen powers which hover about his figures or which act through them are the *ananke*, the *fatum* of ancient Greece, or the terrifying power of Jehovah. The religious spirit of Michelangelo manifests itself in a first period inspired by antiquity—antique in the double sense, both Greek and Jewish. The phases of his own religious development repeat those of the religious evolution of all humanity. During this phase, when his religion is that of the ancients, his Christian and pagan types are interchangeable: a Virgin is transformed into a Sibyl,[4] and a little antique *putto* into the infant Jesus.[5] The *Last Judgment* takes as its point of departure the fall of Phaeton. Christ the Judge is an Apollo, and the Virgin is a crouching Venus.[6]

We tried in the preceding chapter to determine, by analysis of some of the works of Michelangelo's youth and maturity, the manner in which he conceived of a philosophical outlook.

The Virgins in his youthful works are shown to be shrouded in an atmosphere of fate: they live with the presentiment of inescapable catastrophe which they await with

(58)

PLATES I, III, IV

stoic composure. Michelangelo's Saints and Prophets are also in the grip of superior forces; a wind is billowing around them, the divine afflatus can be read on their faces, in their violent gestures, and in their garments: this is the ancient pre-Christian ecstasy. These philosophical attitudes are of religious origin. Already in antiquity, Woman was identified with the *Terra Mater* and endowed with the prescience of death. This idea applied to the Virgin reappeared in the preachers of the Italian Middle Ages. Bernardino da Siena, for instance, claimed that she possessed the prophetic sense to the highest degree.[7] The popular preachers of the fifteenth century repeated this contention in their sermons, and it found powerful expression in Savonarola. In one of his Sermons of 1494 (No. 43) Savonarola said: "The Virgin was illuminated even more than the other prophets by the prophetic light, and that is why she knew in advance that the Child was to suffer his Passion as a human being." [8] This is the thought that Michelangelo expresses in the Virgins of his youth. The first one, *The Virgin of the Steps*, is dated about two years earlier than this sermon. Consequently one cannot say with certainty that Michelangelo was directly influenced by the Dominican.[9] Nevertheless this parallelism is important and is explained by affinities in their thinking. On the other hand, direct contact with Savonarola must certainly have reinforced Michelangelo's own first conceptions.

The pagan element in the religion of the young Michelangelo could have found no better nourishment than the sermons of Savonarola. Indeed, the latter's prophetic side was much more pronounced than his evangelistic side. Condivi,[10] our only witness to Michelangelo's relationship with the great Dominican, said that Michelangelo read and studied the Holy Scriptures, the Old Testament as well as the New, with great attention; that he read also those who had interpreted them, like Savonarola, for whom he always had a great affection

(59)

PLATES VI, X, I

and whose ringing voice ("viva voce") remained in his memory. Vasari, in his first edition, does not mention Savonarola, but in the second (p. 249) he inserts a statement which is evidently inspired by Condivi.[11]

Quite possibly Michelangelo heard the sermons preached by Savonarola between 1493 and 1494 in Santa Maria del Fiore, the subjects of which were the Apocalypse, the first epistle of St. John, the lamentations of Jeremiah, and Genesis. He must have been moved by the Dominican's purity of soul, by the ardor with which he devoted himself to his ideals, by his asceticism, and above all by his vein of prophecy—for all these qualities could be found in the artist himself.

The language of Savonarola's sermons was that of the prophets of the Old Testament, full of violence, calls for repentance, threats of imminent punishment. Savonarola spoke out, without mincing words, against the Church and the corruption of the clergy. He sharply criticized the immorality of Florentine life. Michelangelo's flight from Florence in 1494—shortly before the arrival of the French king Charles VIII's army—could very well have been a consequence of the impression left by Savonarola's sermons predicting the coming of the divine scourge, the appearance of a new Cyrus who would punish Italy and the Church, and the imminence of a new Flood. Michelangelo fled first to Venice, remained there for a short time, then went on to Bologna. There he was commissioned to complete the tomb of St. Dominic by adding three statuettes. He must have esteemed it a great honor to carry out this task, for this monument was erected to the founder of the order to which Savonarola belonged, as did his own eldest brother, Lionardo, another admirer of the great preacher. It may be the influence of Savonarola's sermons that we see in the conception of these three statuettes, which were to finish the monument begun by Niccolò Pisano and his pupils and continued by Niccolò dell'Arca. Instead of

(60)

PLATE XXVIII

following his predecessor dell'Arca's style by making calm and serene figures, full of sweet humility, Michelangelo conceived figures full of passion: St. Proculus, St. Petronius, and the kneeling Angel look like sentinels aware of their sacred mission, which is to watch over the tomb. It should not be forgotten that before going to Florence Savonarola spent seven years in Bologna, from 1475 to 1482, in the very monastery where Michelangelo was then working, and where the memory of the Brother must still have been vivid.

In the meantime Piero de' Medici (successor to Lorenzo) had been expelled from Florence and Savonarola had become master. In June 1495, a new Republic was established in Florence, which followed the religious and political ideas of Savonarola. It was a Christian republic and Jesus Christ was its invisible King. Its constitution, although based on that of Venice, was entirely religious in spirit. Under Savonarola's influence, the tenor of life in Florence changed appreciably. Luxury was abandoned and a sudden puritanism took its place. The party supporting the Dominican monk, the *piagnoni*, triumphed over his enemies, the *arrabbiati*. As proof of the admiration Michelangelo bore Savonarola, he returned to Florence as soon as the Republic was established. Although he was in agreement with the principles of the new Republic, he could not remain there long. Because the Signoria, which was now puritan in spirit, offered him no commissions he made only two little statuettes of children (a San Giovannino and a Cupid, both now lost) during the six months he passed in Savonarola's Republic. In the summer of 1496, he was forced to go to Rome to look for commissions.[12] He worked there for Jacopo Galli, the banker, and for Cardinal Jean de Villiers de la Groslay. It is very probable that Michelangelo did not have any connection with the papal court during this sojourn. Indeed the center of the anti-Savonarola movement was located there under Alexander VI—a movement headed

(61)

PLATE VI

by Fra Mariano da Genazzano, an Augustinian, who declared it his opinion that Savonarola was a withered heretic.[13] Although it is true that the three figures for the tomb of Saint Dominic and certain sibylline Virgins of the early period betray the influence of Savonarola's exalted prophetic spirit, yet some of Michelangelo's other works, done at almost the same time, demonstrate that he was quite able to maintain his artistic independence. Savonarola preached against the imitation of pagan art and against the representation of nude figures; nevertheless Michelangelo executed a *Cupid* (lost) and a *Bacchus* (Bargello), both pagan subjects and both nudes, during Savonarola's government. Michelangelo did the *Bacchus* in Rome at almost the same moment as the Vanities were being burned in Florence at Savonarola's order. On the other hand the contract for the *Pietà* in St. Peter's is dated three months after Savonarola's tragic death on May 23, 1498. When Michelangelo began to work on the group he may perhaps still have been influenced by this event. The iconographic type which he used was the Nordic type of Pietà, which since the middle of the thirteenth century had appeared in French and German miniatures, and which in the course of the fifteenth had spread in Italy. The fundamental theme of every Pietà before Michelangelo's was the *Compassio Mariae,* where the weeping Virgin is holding in her lap the stiff corpse of her son. Michelangelo altered the meaning of the group, accentuating not the Virgin's grief but her acceptance of fate: the death of her son is the fulfillment of a divine decree. Michelangelo's Virgin does not cry; she merely bows her head; and, with a restrained gesture of her hand, expressing obedience to a superior will, she yields to destiny. Now harmony is established between the form of the Virgin and the flexible body of Christ, who seems to sleep in his mother's lap.

Among the Florentine artists, Botticelli, Lorenzo di Credi,

PLATES VII, III

Fra Bartolommeo, and Simone Cronaca were on Savonarola's side. They followed his doctrines, but the spirit dominating their works, except for Botticelli's last productions, was still traditional—that devotion filled with humility which is typical of the Middle Ages still found expression there.

Michelangelo seems to have been the only one among them in whom the Dominican's ardent words aroused a profound echo. The prophetic spirit of Savonarola was so close to Michelangelo's own that the master long remained faithful to it and it periodically appears in his works—in the Prophets, the Sibyls, and the *Flood* of the Sistine Ceiling, in the *Moses* of the Tomb of Julius II, and in the apocalyptic vision of the *Last Judgment.*

Savonarola also preached the necessity for a moral reform of Christianity. In 1496 he said: "All is become venal in the Church; in Rome they sell even the blood of the Lord." This idea of Church reform germinated in the mind of Michelangelo, as we shall see, and he used the same expression in a poem written in 1512 (Frey, *Dicht.* X: "Qui si fa elmi . . .").

It was only when he was about forty-five years old that the pagan spirit in Michelangelo's religious works gradually began to give way to a Christian one. In the *Christ* of Santa Maria sopra Minerva and in the *Virgin* of the Medici Chapel, the divine afflatus and the presentiment of fate yield to a serene evangelical conception. Nevertheless, the form of these works is still influenced by the ancients; Christ is an Apollo, the Virgin a Demeter.

Michelangelo's contract (Milanesi, p. 641) stipulated the execution of "a life-sized marble figure of Christ, naked, standing, holding a cross in his arms, in whatever pose the artist judged to be suitable." Michelangelo fulfilled his commitment for a naked, standing figure holding a cross; to the cross he added the other instruments of the Passion: the

(63)

PLATE XIII

sponge, the lance, and the cord. But the pose, in regard to which the contract gave him complete liberty, could hardly be called conventional. His Christ does not display his wounds. This is the naked figure of an Apollo of noble proportions and beautifully modeled torso, especially at the back; he is standing in *contrapposto*, holding at his right side, in his two hands, the instruments of the Passion, pushing the cross slightly back with his right leg and turning his head in the opposite direction. As in several of Michelangelo's earlier works, such as the *David* or the *Moses*, the two sides of the body are different. The right side (which according to medieval belief is protected by God) has closed contours: this is where he is hiding the instruments of the Passion; the left side (from which evil comes) is open, and it is toward this side that his head is turned.[14]

Here we have a new conception of the Savior, enduring and concealing his suffering behind a noble serenity. The instruments of the Passion which he is concealing from the crowd are the embodiment of Christ's fate. The man and his destiny are here indissolubly linked, and they confront the world in utter loneliness. This loneliness and this stoic attitude, this self-identification with destiny, can be better understood from the poem just mentioned (Frey, *Dicht.* X), in which the artist criticized the corrupt, avaricious, and secularized Church, and the practice of simony. In an emphatic contrast to the Antichrist, who was adored in the Rome of that time, where "the Savior's blood was sold in the hollow of a hand" (*el sangue di Cristo si vend' a giumelle*), where "helmets and swords were fashioned from chalices" (*Qui si fa elmi di calici e spade*), where "the cross and the thorns became lances and shields" (*e croce e spine son lance e rotelle*), Michelangelo tried to erect the image of the true Christ, the Christ of goodness, of suffering and patience. So this statue, in a Roman church of the time, had a special meaning: it was a sort of monument commemorating the true Christ in the midst of the greedy and perverted city. Savonarola's ideas for the internal reform of the Church came to life again. Let us not forget that the statue was made for Santa Maria sopra Minerva, the Dominican church in Rome.

The *Medici Virgin* is no longer an austere sibyl sitting erect, gazing into the distance, absorbed by her vision of destiny and unheeding of the Child. She is the tender virgin mother, who lives only for her son, toward whom she is bending her body to give her milk, in a gesture suffused with maternal love. The child suckling at her breast seems to grow into a little Hercules, while his mother becomes more and more emaciated.

From these two statues, the *Christ of the Minerva* and the *Medici Virgin,* emerge the first signs of a change in Michelangelo's religious thought and feeling. Although executed in the master's Platonic period, the statues anticipate his future conversion. They are still stamped with sublime nobility, yet they already possess the tenderness of the last works.[15]

It is astonishing to find that Michelangelo, after portraying in these two works the Christ and the Virgin discreetly isolating themselves from the faithful, goes on to present ostentatiously, in a little group of works done mostly for Vittoria Colonna, the greatness of the sacrifice of Jesus Christ.[16]

In the *Pietà* which he executed for Vittoria Colonna the master revised his iconography.[17] The group dealing with the same subject in St. Peter's, which he had done in his youth, is a traditional composition: the dead Christ is stretched on the Virgin's knees; the emphasis is on the Virgin. But in the *Pietà* for Vittoria Colonna, all the emphasis is placed on Christ. His body becomes the center of the composition. He is presented to the viewer in a vertical position between the Virgin's knees and supported by two angels; the Virgin is ex-

(65)

PLATES XV, XLIII

pressing her grief in a despairing gesture, and seems to be calling attention to the immensity of the sacrifice. The same idea is repeated in the inscription on the cross, which is taken from Dante's *Paradiso:* "Non vi si pensa quanto sangue costa" (No one thinks of how much blood this is costing). Michelangelo seemingly reached this new solution by integrating the theme of the Pietà into a traditional representation of the Holy Trinity.[18] The harmonious beauty of the first *Pietà* is lost in the second interpretation; this one has a rigid abstract symmetry and an almost geometric regularity. It is no longer a human situation that the artist is interpreting, but a religious symbol.

The innovations which he incorporated into the Crucifixion executed about 1540 are analogous.[19] Whereas Renaissance tradition represented the crucified Christ as already dead, Michelangelo showed him still alive, his body twisted, his eyes turned pathetically toward heaven, recommending his spirit to the Father, as Vasari puts it (1568, p. 249).[20] The two angels, like echoes of his sorrows, are crying beside him. Before that the angels' function had been to catch the blood of Christ in chalices, and not to express his sorrow.

In a Holy Family, a red chalk drawing of the beginning of this period, called *Il Silenzio,* the Infant Jesus and not the Virgin is again the center of the picture.[21] Lying on his holy mother's lap, the Infant Jesus is the object of the adoration and meditation of the Holy Family: the Virgin, St. Joseph, and little St. John are all watching him, as if they can already foresee his mission and his fate; in the background the silhouettes of some angels are lightly indicated; the Child's outstretched attitude recalls that of the first *Pietà,* so that even he himself is anticipating his future. Again this is not a historical scene but rather symbolizes all the adoration ever bestowed upon the Savior.

Michelangelo thus emphasized the sacrifice of Christ

(66)

PLATES XLII, XLIII

throughout, even at the expense of the organic unity of his compositions; one may ask what led the master to this new conception.

As we know, the *Pietà* and the *Crucifixion* were executed for Vittoria Colonna. This lady, a descendant of one of the oldest patrician families in Italy, was not just one of the most cultivated personalities of the Renaissance; at that time she belonged to a religious movement called the "Italian Reform." This movement was distinguished from the contemporary Reformation in the North by its desire to realize its ends within the framework of the Catholic Church.[22]

After Savonarola's death his disciples had continued the struggle for the internal reform of the Church. The purification of the Church was the main objective of the Council of Pisa (1511) and the Fifth Lateran Council (1512). At the Lateran Council, Pico della Mirandola launched his appeal to Leo X to bring about internal reform. Other religious spirits had founded in Rome in 1513 the "Oratory of Divine Love" (Oratorium Divini Amoris), with the same intention of renewing the faith. Several of its members, Sadoleto, Ghiberti, Carafa (later Paul IV), were to play a considerable role in the Reform movement and the Counter Reformation. After 1527 (*sacco di Roma*) the Oratory of Divine Love was dissolved. Most of its members fled to Venice, where they met other notable ecclesiastics—Cortesi, Priuli, Contarini, and Pole.

Eight years later, several members of this group were made cardinals by Paul III and constituted the "Consilium de emendanda Ecclesia." But between times the Northern Reform movement penetrated to Naples with the arrival of Juan de Valdés.

Juan de Valdés came from Spain about 1531 and lived in Rome until 1534, then in Naples, where he died in 1541. Before his departure for Italy Valdés had followed the teachings of Erasmus, as Marcel Bataillon's research shows.[23] He based his belief on St. Paul's sentence: "Therefore we conclude that a man is justified by faith without the deeds of the law" (Romans III, 28). This was an idea already expressed by Savonarola in his *Trattato dell' Umiltà*, which was a point of departure for the doctrine of justification by faith alone.

A little circle of cultured men and women, mostly of noble birth and from high ecclesiastical and lay society, formed around Valdés. Ochino, the greatest of the Italian preachers, was soon an ardent propagator of these new ideas. After Valdés' death in 1541, the circle in Naples moved to Viterbo, to the cloister of Santa Caterina, which was dominated by the figure of Cardinal Reginald Pole. In this circle at Viterbo could be found Flamini, Carnesecchi, Vittorio Soranzo, Alvise Priuli, and Vittoria Colonna.

The essential doctrine in the beliefs of this group was a new conception of salvation. Valdés and his circle, probably influenced by the Reformation in the North, believed in justification through faith in the suffering and death of the Savior. This doctrine was a spiritualization and a transmutation of the dogma of salvation in the subjective sense.[24] The emphasis, which until then had been placed on the objective fact of the *infusio gratiae* of the Sacraments by the priest, was now transferred to the soul's behavior in its relation to the sacrifice of Christ. The theory held that grace depended on man's faith, that grace was mainly a function of the soul. The radical way in which this new doctrine was sustained is demonstrated by a little book, then very popular in Italy, entitled *Del beneficio di Gesù Cristo crocifisso verso i Cristiani* (published anonymously, but written by Fra Benedetto da Mantua), where one can find the following sentence on Justification: "The justice of Christ will be sufficient to make us just and to make us children of grace, without any good works on our part, works which can only be good if, before carrying them out, we are made good and just ourselves through faith, as St. Augustine says." If until then grace had been obtained by the sacramental infusion carried out by the priest, the infusion of an objective substance into the soul considered as a passive vessel, henceforth the whole accent was on the active faith of the soul in Christ's sacrifice. That is to say, grace was dependent on the dynamic and subjective act of the believing soul.

Like all the other members of Valdés' circle, Vittoria Colonna adhered to this doctrine, as her poems prove. It is elaborated in sonnet LII of her *Canzoniere:*

> *Con la croce, col sangue e col sudore,*
> *Con lo spirto al periglio ognor più ardente,*
> *E non con voglie pigre ed opre lente,*
> *Dee l'uom servire al suo vero Signore.*

(Man must serve his true Lord, not by indolent intentions and tardy good works, but by the cross, by blood and sweat, by his ardent spirit always prepared for danger.)

Another still more striking example can be found in sonnet XXXI:

> *Il Padre Eterno del ciel . . . vuol la nostra*
> *Virtù solo per fede.*

(The eternal Father in heaven . . . desires our virtue by faith alone.)

When Valdés came to live in Naples in 1534, Vittoria Colonna was about to leave Ischia. It is not known whether she met Valdés; if she did not, she could certainly have got to know his ideas through Ochino, who was her spiritual director from 1534 to 1541. After 1541 this role was taken over by Cardinal Reginald Pole.

The position adopted by Vittoria Colonna concerning justification by faith alone was submitted to the tribunal of the

Inquisition by Carnesecchi. Carnesecchi [25] said that the Marchesa attributed great importance to the doctrine, but that at the same time she showed by her life and example (almsgiving and charities) that she also attached great importance to "good works," and in this attitude she was following the counsels of Cardinal Pole: "[Vittoria Colonna] attribuiva molto alla gratia et alla fede in suoi ragionamenti. Et d'altra parte nella vita et nelle attioni sue mostrava di tenere gran conto dell'opere facendo grande elemosine et usando charità universalmente con tutti, nel che veniva a . . . seguire il consiglio [del] Cardinale [Pole] . . . cioè che ella dovesse attendere a credere come se per la fede sola s'havesse a salvare, et d'altra parte attendere ad operare come se la salute sua consistesse nelle opere . . ." (Vittoria Colonna attributed a great deal of importance to grace and faith in her reasoning. And by her life and acts she showed that she had a high opinion of good works, distributing many alms and spreading charity everywhere, following in this the advice of the Cardinal [Pole], who said that she must believe that she would attain salvation by faith alone, but that she should behave as if her salvation depended on good works.) This compromise permitted the reconciliation of both the inner and the outer, of tradition and the Reform of the Church. Michelangelo's attitude was similar.

The friendship between Vittoria Colonna and Michelangelo probably began in the autumn of 1538. [26] That year Vittoria Colonna was living in the convent of San Silvestro in Capite, in Rome. The two met every Sunday, at San Silvestro al Monte Cavallo, and discussed religious problems. Michelangelo seems to have acquired from Vittoria Colonna the doctrine of "justification by faith alone," and consequently he must have abandoned the idea of freedom of will and turned to the idea of God acting through man. In one of his letters, probably written in 1540, addressed to the Marchesa Colonna,

Michelangelo said: "ho riconosciuto e visto che la grazia di Iddio non si puo comperare e che'l tenerla a disagio è peccato grandissimo." [27] (I now understand and see that the grace of God cannot be bought, and that it is a very great sin to find this grace oppressive.)

In a sonnet to Vittoria Colonna (Frey, *Dicht.* CIX, 97), Michelangelo cries out:

> *Chieggio a voi, alta e diva Donna,*
> *Saper, se'n ciel men grado tiene*
> *L'umil pecchato che'l superchio bene.*

(I beg you, oh divine and noble woman, to tell me if in Heaven the humbly acknowledged sin is worth less than the supreme good [that is, than good works].)

We find this doctrine of justification by faith in a whole series of poems from the artist's last period:

> *O carne, o sangue, o legnio, o doglia strema,*
> *Giusto per vo' si facci el mio peccato.*
>
> (Frey, *Dicht.* XLVIII)

(Oh flesh, oh blood, oh cross, oh suffering in extremis, grant that my sins be justified in your eyes.)

> *Tuo sangue [Signor] sol mie colpe lavi e tochi.*
>
> (Frey, *Dicht.* CLII)

(Only your blood, Lord, can wash me and cleanse me of my sins.)

The same thought is expressed again in (Frey, *Dicht.* CLXV):

> *Col tuo sangue l'alma purghi e sani,*
> *Dal infinite colpe e moti humani.*

(With your blood you cleanse the soul and heal it of the infinite vices and human desires.)

(71)

The idea that good works do not represent a personal merit in man, but come from God acting in him, is expressed in this verse (Frey, *Dicht.* CLIV):

Tu sol [Signor] se' seme d'opre caste e pie.
(You alone [Lord] are the seed of pure and pious works.)

This conception goes back to St. Augustine and was being sustained at that time in the very bosom of the Church at the Council of Trent, as has been pointed out by Jean Baruzi.[28] So it is not to be attributed solely to Luther's Reformation.

All these verses prove that Michelangelo knew the doctrine of justification by faith in the sacrifice of Christ, and this explains why he revised the iconography of the works done for Vittoria Colonna, which we have just been discussing, and put all the emphasis on the divine sacrifice.

None of the adherents of this religious movement felt that there was a contradiction between the doctrine of justification by faith alone and the postulate of good works.[29] To them the two doctrines were complementary. Cardinal Contarini, one of Valdés' most important disciples, said of the theme of justification: "No one does good in order to obtain grace, but because he has already received it. How indeed can anyone who has not already been justified live as a just man? So the most important element is grace; the good works come afterwards." Here Contarini was speaking entirely in the spirit of the Reformation. In spite of this, he remained in the bosom of the Church. Cardinal Pole was even nearer to Protestantism in the matter of justification by faith alone, as can be seen from one of his letters (*Ep.* IV, 53). Nevertheless it was he who gave Vittoria Colonna the advice mentioned earlier. The same is true of Vergerio and Carnesecchi.

None of them wanted to join one of the reformed churches, and if later some of them left the Catholic

Church, this was only because the Holy Office gave them no choice. They were compelled either to abjure their religious convictions or to be branded as heretics. Only the insistence of the Holy See, by forcing them to declare themselves unequivocally, made them conscious of the contradiction between their convictions and the dogmas of the Catholic Church. The most striking example of this was Ochino. He remained within the bosom of the Church until the ultimate limit. Not until he saw clearly that the Church would not accept him and was hounding him, did he separate himself from it. The scission is clearly explained in a letter he wrote to Vittoria Colonna.[30]

Nor did Michelangelo see any contradiction between the new attitude and the traditional doctrines. On the one hand, writing to his nephew he advocated the usual doctrine of good works carried out for the soul's salvation; on the other, in his poetry he expressed the new doctrine of justification by faith alone. *Fides* and *Caritas* are sisters; they are two movements of a soul already justified; one, *Fides* (Rachel), in an upward *élan* ascends to God; the other, *Caritas* (Leah), is a downward movement toward the world, resulting from the abundance of a soul through which God is operating. Indeed, in the *Rachel* and the *Leah,* two statues which Michelangelo executed for the Tomb of Julius II, he showed Faith and Charity as sisters in this sense. These two statues were executed between 1543 and 1545 for the last version of the tomb of Julius II, which version is visible proof of Michelangelo's religious conversion. The tomb is no longer a diagram of the hierarchies of the world, as were the projects before it, but a purely religious monument. In fact, Michelangelo suppressed the triumphal symbols: for the Slaves he substituted volutes, and for the Victories, Rachel and Leah, who personify the contemplative life (*Fides*) and the active life (*Caritas*), that is, the two kinds of religious life on earth. Above them is the

(73)

PLATE XIX

Pope, half lying on his sarcophagus, with an expression of reverie on his face. Above him appear the Virgin and Child. To his right and left are a Prophet and a Sibyl. The two zones of the monument are linked by a rotary movement like that in the *Last Judgment*. Instead of the objective hierarchies of the universe, we are confronted with the Pope's subjective vision of the afterlife.

During the pontificates of Pope Julius III and Paul IV Carafa (1555–59), the "Italian Reform" movement was practically suppressed. New religious movements sprang into life, among the most important of them Ignatius Loyola's Society of Jesus. Loyola had in common with the Italian reformers an ardent desire to cleanse the Church of its impurities and to revive the faith. He differed from them only in the ways in which he tried to attain this end. This explains why Michelangelo, ten years after embracing the ideas of the Valdés circle, could offer his services to Ignatius Loyola. A letter from Loyola to the Conde de Melito, dated July 21, 1554, informs us that Michelangelo had offered a year earlier, out of pure devotion and without compensation, to direct the building of the new church of the order of Loyola, the Gesù.[31] A plan by Michelangelo for the Gesù was mentioned in 1554. A red chalk drawing of it still exists in the Uffizi and has been identified by A. E. Popp;[32] it shows a broad and relatively short longitudinal church with one main, probably barrel-vaulted, nave and lateral chapels, a plan reminiscent of that of San Andrea in Mantua. This idea inspired Vignola in 1568 when he executed the projects for the famous church of the Gesù, which was to become the prototype of the innumerable churches of the Counter Reformation all over Europe. Thus it was Michelangelo and not Vignola who was the real creator of the Jesuit type of church.

The profound piety of the artist in his old age knew nothing of the antinomy existing between the dogmas of the

Church and the new doctrines. His main problem was to obtain grace through divine love. Sometimes he felt himself filled with an ardent faith; sometimes he felt abandoned by God. In his works he embodied these two extreme states of soul: the ecstasy and the feeling of separation from God. The most poignant expression of the feeling of separation occurs in the sonnets; his last works of art are true visions expressing the fusion of his spirit with the divine love.

He seems always to have written his religious poems in what he called the intervals ("intervalli," Frey, *Dicht.* XCVII) during which God abandoned him. These poems were conceived in the suffering engendered by periods of waiting for religious inspiration. The hymns to the Lord, the praise of heaven, the joy of a soul filled with God, all these are missing from his *Canzoniere spirituale.* These poems are simply expressions of remorse and repentance, or they are prayers, or else they are despairing cries for divine help (Frey, *Dicht.* CLI): "Non è più bassa, o vil cosa terrena che quel che, senza te, mi sento e sono." (There is nothing on earth lower and more vile than what I feel myself to be and what I am without you, [Lord].)

The religious ardor, what Michelangelo calls "l'interno ardore che mi leva di terra" (Frey, *Dicht.* XCVII), is always described in these poems as belonging to the past or the future. He suffers profoundly from being so rarely visited by it. Michelangelo questions his own feelings, reproaches himself for not possessing true faith and not being sincere with himself. A cry for help breaks from him; he asks God to help him believe (Frey, *Dicht.* CXL): "Vorrei voler, Signor, quel ch' io non voglio . . ." (I would like, Lord, to want what I do not want . . .)

Often his poems describe the repentance of a soul which, in contemplating its past, recognizes that it has lived a life of error, has wasted time in the adoration of vain idols—

among which idols he now places his own art—when it should have been concentrating on that which alone can bring salvation, the contemplation of God. (Frey, *Dicht.* CXLVII, CL; cf. also CXLVIII, CLV, CLVI)

Petrarch's sonnet 365 was Michelangelo's model for the content and form of these poems.[33] It is interesting to compare his poetry with Petrarch's. The light, musical language of the latter is replaced by the sculptor's heavy rhythms. Whereas every line of Petrarch has its own balance, in Michelangelo's poetry one movement flows from line to line, running through the whole composition in a crescendo, like an avalanche gathering strength as it rushes downwards: as for example in the poem "Giunto è gia il corso della vita mia . . ." (Frey, *Dicht.* CXLVII). This is the torrent of Michelangelo's soul in its search for God, a torrent whose violence gives to each of its elements a color and meaning different from that which they would have by themselves.

These poems, which have a depth of thought, a dynamism, and a gravity of style quite new to the Italian poetry of the sixteenth century, are visible evidence of Michelangelo's conversion. More and more, religious thoughts take possession of his spirit. All other thoughts now seem vain to him.

In his last plastic works, the series beginning about 1550, Michelangelo succeeded in creating forms which were the appropriate expression of his religious feeling. It might be said that he was now creating a religious style whereas the works he had made for Vittoria Colonna were still in the heroic mold. These religious works will be analyzed from a plastic standpoint in the next chapter, where the master's artistic conceptions are discussed. For the moment we will concentrate on the religious conceptions from which they originated.

They are true incarnations of mystic visions of the divine, born of spiritual effort (*meditatio*) and having as their aim the elevation of the artist's soul above his instincts. It does seem as if the aged Michelangelo considered the furnishing of his soul with these inner images to be a means of reaching salvation. They offer striking resemblances, even in their outer form, to the religious visions of every age, as these are known from the descriptions of mystics or the works of art of certain great religious painters.[34]

This transformation in Michelangelo's art comes to light in the series of drawings representing Christ on the Cross between the Virgin and St. John, which can be dated, according to their style, between 1550 and 1556.[35] The crucial point of these compositions is not the Christ and his suffering but the human feelings which are aroused by the death of the Lord, and which are embodied in the sorrowful figures at the foot of the Cross. The real purpose of the drawings is to show how the Crucifixion is reflected in the conscience of Michelangelo and of man in general. Above all the master underlines, just as he does in his poems, the remorse, the feeling of guilt, and the weight of responsibility which the human race bears for this crime.

In the drawing in Oxford (Ashmolean Museum), the two figures below the Cross, probably centurions, look as though they were fleeing in horror from the place of agony. Stephaton is holding his head in his hands as if he cannot realize what has happened, and Longinus looks like a murderer pursued by his own remorse. They seem to share in the responsibility for the crime which has been perpetrated.

In another drawing, in Windsor Castle, Mary and St. John appear to be cast down by their burden of sin. Shivering, the Virgin hugs her arms to her breast and hides her face, while St. John trembles in the expectation of punishment. It really seems as if Michelangelo were deliberately trying to convey feelings not only of sadness and sorrow but of horror, fear, and despair. Indeed, he chose to portray these two figures in

PLATE XLIV

the same attitudes as two of the figures in the *Last Judgment* —the young man with raised hands, high on the left side of the fresco, and the Virgin—both of whom are expressing unequivocal feelings of terror.

In one of the last drawings of this group, now in London (British Museum), the feeling of fear and despair is at last overcome. Mary and St. John are pressing against the legs of Christ, as if seeking in his presence the cure for their despair. They feel safe beneath the arms of the crucified Savior spread over them like a protecting canopy. The death of Christ now assumes its full significance as the symbol of the redemption of humanity through grace.

Several other drawings demonstrate this same evolution of the master's thought. For instance, there is an *Annunciation,* in Oxford (Ashmolean Museum), which can be dated after 1556, thanks to an inscription on the same sheet.[36] It is the interpretation of an event which is wholly spiritual. The heavy Virgin is sitting motionless. Before her appears, like a vision, a light and incorporeal being, hovering above the ground and seemingly come from afar.[37] The different degrees of reality which these two figures represent are emphasized even more by the differences in the type of drawing and proportions which Michelangelo elected to use for each one. The announcement of the birth of the Savior awakens in the Virgin a wave of entirely inner emotions of which the angel is the ethereal manifestation; this is the real subject of the composition.

One drawing, traced with a trembling hand, perhaps the last to come down to us from Michelangelo (London, British Museum), represents the Virgin and Child. Gauche, her body roughly sketched with many *pentimenti,* her knees slightly bent, she seems to be quite naked; but actually a transparent veil flows around her body. She is holding the Child tenderly and he is kissing his mother's cheek. A return

(78)

to primitive Eve, this is a vision, free of all irrelevancy, of Woman and maternal love. The Virgin's body seems to shine with a soft radiance, and the faint, indecisive lines of the chalk enveloping it in a light halo help to accentuate its dreamlike character.

The renunciation of plastic modeling revealed here is the most refined and consistent expression of Michelangelo's late spirituality. It explains the rarity of the sculptures executed by the artist at this period of his life. Indeed the plastic art, because of its material and technique, is much less suited to the interpretation of such transparent visions. And of course, Michelangelo was no longer able to carve with the same ease and precision as in former years.

Nevertheless Michelangelo tried it in the only two sculptures which he executed during the last twenty years of his life.

Like the *Pietà* for Vittoria Colonna, the *Deposition* (called "Pietà") of the Cathedral of Florence derives from the Trinity type: the body is supported vertically on both sides under the armpits, while a fourth figure dominates the group behind the Christ.[38] But the role of the two angels is assumed here by the Virgin and Mary Magdalene, the Virgin's place being occupied by the hooded figure of Joseph of Arimathea, an auto-portrait of the artist, according to Vasari, who calls the figure Nicodemus. Vasari says also (letter to Lionardo Buonarroti of March 18, 1564) that the group was intended for Michelangelo's own tomb. The abstract and rather rigid symmetry of the composition meant for Vittoria Colonna, which is inscribed within a hexagon, becomes a group full of life and suppleness, with closely knit figures, whose general shape is that of a slender cone. The master tried to attenuate as much as possible the material effect of the bodies: they no longer have the massive forms of his statuary. Thin, slender, almost skeletal, they are presented to the viewer, not full-face,

(79)

PLATE XX

but from a narrow angle. The twisted body of Christ seems to be sliding toward the ground, and Mary, her eyes closed, her face transfigured by supernatural bliss, is receiving him into her arms. Their two heads are touching, and that of the Mother serves as support for the head of Jesus Christ. Joseph of Arimathea tenderly holds the right arm of the body and seems to be pushing it toward Mary, as he lays his left hand on her back in a protective gesture. As the personification of divine providence, he accomplishes with profound emotion that reunion of mother and son desired by Mary. Human grief seems to be surpassed. The living characters are filled with the same feeling of beatitude that is traced on the refined and serene features of the dead Christ. The individual forms seem to interpenetrate like the feelings of the characters. Each figure is but a nuance of the eternal bliss which results from participation in divine love.

The *Pietà* formerly in the Palazzo Rondanini in Rome, and now in the Castello Sforzesco in Milan, is not mentioned either in Vasari's first edition or in Condivi.[39] In his second edition, Vasari reports that after having mutilated the Cathedral Pietà, Michelangelo returned to a block in which he had once sketched a Pietà. A letter from Daniele da Volterra (G. Daelli, *Carte Michelangiolesche inedite* [Milan, 1865], p. 34) informs us that Michelangelo was working on this group six days before his death. The preliminary sketches on the Oxford Sheet can be dated, according to their style, between 1550 and 1556. Therefore the first version of this marble composition must go back to the same period; and the artist must have reworked the upper section of the group in the last year of his life. He abolished the antithesis between the passive weight of the corpse and the effort made by the living figure of the Virgin. The slender body of Christ, which cannot be held up by his legs since they are giving way, still rises, conquering the laws of gravity, while the figure of Mary

PLATES XXVII, XXI

seeks support by leaning against him and seems to draw from his inert body the warmth of life. The two bodies are so closely united that they merge into one another, and their forms are hardly differentiated. Indeed, in the last version Michelangelo carved the body of Christ from what had been the Virgin's body in the earlier versions.

Once more Michelangelo subordinated physical beauty to the inner radiance of the soul. The shapes of these two bodies appear singularly poor and devoid of all physical perfection. Their outline is angular and rectilinear, and their surface— except in the parts done previously and not retouched—offers the rough treatment already used by Michelangelo in the Florentine *Deposition* to attenuate the too apparent contrasts of light and shade, and to make the inner light stand out mysteriously.

The feeling of religious beatitude which Michelangelo achieved in his last works was not born of the candid assurance of a man of the Middle Ages, nor of an ecstatic discipline artificially cultivated (as in the Counter Reformation). In profound solitude, beyond the world and the Church, Michelangelo sought alone the road which would lead him to beatitude. It is those long soul-searchings and those long gropings which give to these works their moving depth. The feeling of bliss seems always to be tinged with the suffering which he endured to attain it.

The drawings and the two "Pietàs" of the last period could be called "Orisons," or inner prayers. The external and material image of Christ is supplanted by the internal spiritual image, directly inspired—as the Italian reformers would say—by the Holy Ghost.[40]

Savonarola had said already in his little book *Della orazione mentale:* "The Lord desires inner worship without regard to external ceremony . . . Ceremony is like medicine for souls which do not have the true fervor." This idea of inner

(81)

PLATE XXVII

worship was expressed again by Valdés in his *Cento e Dieci Divine Considerazioni* (No. 63), and the passage clarifies once more the plastic character of Michelangelo's last works. It says that the image of the Crucified Christ should evoke in the soul the suffering of Christ. Once the soul has attained this suffering, the eyes of the body turn away from the external representation and the eyes of the spirit concentrate on the inner image of suffering.

Belief is no longer based on the "story" which recounts the suffering, but on the "revelation" which unveils it: as Valdés himself says, not on the *relazione* but on the *revelazione*.

CHAPTER

IV

Michelangelo's Artistic Convictions

MICHELANGELO's pupil and biographer Condivi mentions that the master wanted "to write an inventive theory, resulting from a long experience." Of what this theory consisted he didn't know exactly, said Condivi, but added, "I do know that when Michelangelo read Albrecht Dürer he found him very feeble, and to tell the truth Albrecht deals only with measurements and the variations of bodies [i.e., age and sex], which really cannot be formulated by means of hard and fast rules . . . , yet he says nothing about what is most important, that is, about human actions and gestures." [1]

Of what then did Michelangelo's theory of art consist? A few scattered observations in his letters, some of his poems, and apart from them the short treatise by one of his indirect pupils, Vincenzo Danti—these are the main clues we have to help us reconstruct it. [2] To be sure, the master's artistic principles can be detected in the works themselves, but it must be kept in mind that theory and practice do not always agree.

According to the artistic theories of the Renaissance, from L. B. Alberti to Leonardo, a work of art should be regarded as an "imitation" of nature.[3] "Imitation of nature" here means, in the first place, imitation of models, in contrast to the custom in workshops of the Middle Ages, where instead of natural objects exemplars were copied. Secondly, it means the imitation of the creative processes of nature. Nature to the Renaissance artists was a cosmos, and the laws which governed it were open to experience and human understanding —but clarified in works of art.

Art was conceived as an instrument for the investigation of the laws of nature—art was a science. It followed therefore that the artist had to be well versed in the fields of mathematics, geometry, physics, mechanics, and philosophy. Science and art were still not differentiated. The modern scientific method had not yet been discovered.

The fundamental problem for an artist in the second half of the fifteenth century was "exactitude," or "accuracy" in the artistic representation of the visible world—exactitude in the rendering of space, in the anatomy and proportions of figures, in the right relationship between the scale of the objects represented and the space around them. Perspective and anatomy were used to give this "accurate" representation of the world.

Michelangelo inherited these Renaissance traditions. A study of his work shows clearly that he regarded a profound knowledge of the anatomy of the human body and of perspective as the obvious premise of artistic creation. However, this knowledge was not for him an end in itself, but only a means to an end. The knowledge he acquired was simply intended to serve the higher purpose of his art, which he conceived as a re-creation of the intelligible world, the "true reality," the οὐσία.

It is possible to deduce from Michelangelo's work his knowledge of perspective and anatomy. From the *Virgin of the Steps*, his first relief, can be established the young artist's knowledge of perspective *dal sotto in sù*. At the top left of the relief the tread of the steps partly hides the legs of the two *putti*. The diminishment of perspective through distance is still rendered in a rather awkward way, by means of the gradual diminishment in size of each step, and of the figures in the background. But the young Michelangelo did not worry about transitions. Instead of constructing a space according to Euclidian optics he used his knowledge of perspective to dispose the planes of the relief distinctly. He determined the three main planes of his relief by means of diminishing perspective. The spatial effect of the whole was subordinated to the effect of the three planes one behind the other. In the *Doni Virgin* he applied his knowledge of perspective in the same way in order to emphasize the planes of the picture. Here too the three planes were clearly separated, so that middle and background would allow the plastic relief of the group in the foreground to stand out more strongly. Only in the *Flood* in the Sistine Ceiling do we notice for the first time a modest attempt to link together the three planes by means of diagonals—but the diagonals are not yet linked to one another: there are still distinct breaks between the three planes of the picture. In the Sistine Ceiling each zone, and within it each Prophet and Sibyl, each history, each triangle and lunette, has its own focal point. As a consequence the dynamic-plastic conception is overwhelmingly more important than the illusionistic effect.

If in these works perspective foreshortening was used for purely plastic purposes, in other works Michelangelo sometimes openly disavowed the laws of foreshortening by distance. He did not intend to represent things as the human eye sees them but as they are in essence; not as they appear

(85)

PLATES I, V

but as they are according to their Idea. In order to counteract the deceptive foreshortening in nature he gave larger dimensions to the more distant figures. Consequently to the viewer they seem equal in size to the nearer figures. Figures receive from this an "objective" quality, so to speak, quite independent of the observer's eye. Only a complete master of perspective could put it aside deliberately as soon as it was unsuited to his purpose and could permit himself, without appearing arbitrary, this reversal of the laws of foreshortening. In the contract for the Piccolomini Monument in Siena, 1504 (Milanesi, p. 617), Michelangelo stipulated that the upper figures of the monument must be a handbreadth larger than the lower ones, "because of their distance from the eye." And in the contract for the Tomb of Julius II, 1513 (Milanesi, p. 637), he stated that in the "Capelletta" at the top of the monument five figures would be placed which would be larger than all the others, and he emphasized: "because they are at a greater distance from the eye." So it is clear that in his maturity Michelangelo worked consciously against the laws of perspective foreshortening.

He followed the same principle in the *Last Judgment*, where the figures of the upper zones are actually larger than those of the lower ones.[4] Here, however, their size is determined as well by the objective meaning and importance which they assume in the *Judgment*. The space of the fresco is not constructed according to the rules of linear perspective but is conceived as being filled with magnetic powers. Instead of the closed static space of the Quattrocento, Michelangelo has created an open dynamic space, suggesting the infinity of the universe.

 We know from Condivi and Vasari that Michelangelo studied anatomy in a scientific way with the help of dissections. In his youth, between 1492 and 1494, his friend the Prior of Santo Spirito in Florence placed corpses at his dis-

(86)

posal. As a token of his gratitude Michelangelo made for the Prior a wooden Christ on the Cross.[5] This crucifix shows the extent of Michelangelo's knowledge of anatomy gathered from his dissections. And we know from his letters and from Condivi that the master in his old age, about 1550, was a close friend of the surgeon and anatomist Realdo Colombo; the two are supposed to have exchanged opinions on anatomy. It is said that the surgeon sent the master a Negro corpse of great beauty. Michelangelo brought this corpse to the neighborhood of Sant' Agata, where he showed Condivi "strange and hidden things about it." Condivi stated that he had taken down Michelangelo's observations with the intention of publishing them, but had never fulfilled this plan.[6]

From Michelangelo's works emerges the fact that he had a profound knowledge of anatomy. But he was not interested in anatomy as a science *per se*—as was Leonardo. Rather it was for him, as was perspective, an auxiliary science, a means to a fundamental knowledge of the structure of the human body, which the artist wanted to re-create in his works, not by copying this or that model, but by grasping the meaning of the human body in its original beauty and in the rhythmic power of its abundant life. This is already quite clear in the naked forms of his *Battle of the Centaurs:* here the thin, stiff Quattrocento figures, already criticized by Leonardo, have disappeared; Michelangelo has filled them with a pulsating inner life.[7] Nevertheless it is a fact worth noting that in the entire works of Michelangelo there is no authenticated anatomical drawing in the narrow sense of the word, where the structure of the skeleton and muscular system as an autonomous and distinct component of the human body is studied—as it was in the anatomical drawings of Leonardo da Vinci.[8] Even Michelangelo's "theoretical" studies of the human body are purely plastic. Obviously he was never able to regard the skeleton as a system which could be detached from

(87)

PLATE II

the whole, when it was a question of representing the living body. Only the unity of the plastic bodily form existed for him, a unity in which the muscles and bones merely indicate the inner powers and tensions of the substance which they shape from within. They are not a hidden static structure inside the body; on the contrary, bones and muscles are forces, and need the body's substance in order to manifest themselves. Away from the complexus of the body they have no life. The blood stream flows through these superhuman forms, and Michelangelo seizes its rhythm—a truly dynamic conception.

In his studies Michelangelo treats form according to its own laws, that is, from the aspect of its original purpose, as nature intends it, before it becomes marred by the vicissitudes of life. The study of a leg, for instance (in Cod. Vat., 3211),[9] imparts the natural idea of the leg as an elastic organ, whose function is to carry the body. The weight of the body demands the curved line of the calf, which is repeated like a slim echo in the ankle and ends in the foot which serves as base. When Michelangelo executed this same leg in the Christ of the *Last Judgment,* he was forced to modify it slightly to suit the movement of the entire figure.

Vincenzo Danti, an indirect pupil of Michelangelo, said in his *Trattato delle perfette proporzioni* (1567) that an artist should not simply copy (*ritrarre*) visible nature but should imitate it (*imitare*) in its purposes; that is to say, he should "imitare la perfetta forma intenzionale della natura." "The perfect form, as nature desires it, is conceived in our spirit, and we must now try to express it in shapes, whether in marble, in color, or in another way." It follows that the artistic *concetto* (the Idea) is the inner image that the artist creates for himself of nature's intentions. The subjective intention of the artist is therefore identified with the objective intention of nature. Benedetto Varchi, in a discourse on one of Michelan-

(88)

PLATE XLII

gelo's poems, which he gave with the artist's permission in the Academy of Florence in 1546, defined the relation of the artistic idea to form in the following way: "Art is but the inner image of the object to be painted, an image that lives in the soul of the artist, that is, in his imagination. This image is the principle which determines the form to be imposed on the material, and so it is the fundamental principle, the *causa efficiens*, of everything created."[10] Varchi also emphasizes the fact that Michelangelo's *concetto* has the same meaning as the Greek *idéa*, the Roman *exemplar*, the Italian *modello*, and that it corresponds to Aristotle's *forma agens*.

This theory, also favored by Michelangelo, transfers the emphasis from the outer to the inner: the visible form is conceived as an emanation of the Idea. It adds a new dimension to the artistic theories of the Renaissance. Before Michelangelo, artists still adhered to Ghiberti's definition: "Ma la proporzionalità solamente fa pulcritudine" (Only proportion results in beauty).[11]

Michelangelo himself sees beauty in the correspondence of form and idea, for "beauty depends on the final purpose." "It is in those elements which best suit their aim and purpose that beauty shines out most strongly." Danti has handed on this passage.[12]

The notion of proportion which until then had been based on the relationships of quantitative measurements was now applied to the qualitative, that is, to showing the correspondence of the external object to the idea within it. This "spiritual proportion" (*misura intellettuale*) is a general rule, which can be applied not only to the human body but to all phenomena of nature. Danti said of a rough piece of marble: "When we see a marble block of shining purity and adequate hardness, then we say that it is put together proportionally, because it fulfills its purpose of being white and hard."

And to cite Danti once more: "Proportion consists in the

exact assimilation of the form to the idea." Consequently there are no fixed quantitative proportions. "The body is in movement from one end to the other, or to express it differently, there are no static proportions . . . all limbs change, as they move, in length and breadth."

We know from other sources (Condivi) that these words of Danti's, rejecting fixed proportions, go back to Michelangelo. Vasari too had noticed that Michelangelo's figures are sometimes nine, sometimes ten, sometimes twelve "heads" high. In fact the *David* of 1504 measures nine, the *Christ of the Minerva* about ten, the *Victory* about twelve "heads" high (length of face).

Michelangelo's successors inform us that the master declined in the name of "spiritual proportion" to make use of the mathematical, that is, quantitative methods which played such a large role in the artistic theories of L. B. Alberti, Leonardo, and Dürer. According to Lomazzo, Michelangelo explained: "All geometry, all arithmetic, and all rules of perspective are useless without the observing eye." [13] Vasari attributed this remark to Michelangelo: "One should have a compass not in his hand but in his eye, for the hand works but the eye judges." [14]

Several times during his life Michelangelo gave expression to the thought, already hinted at by L. B. Alberti, that artistic activity springs from the mind and not from manual dexterity: "One paints with the brain and not with the hands," he said. So he found quite senseless the dispute of his contemporaries over the superiority of painting or sculpture. Leonardo represented the opinion that painting is superior to sculpture. In opposition, Michelangelo, writing to Varchi, says (Milanesi, p. 522): "I understand by sculpture what is created by removal, *per forza di levare;* what comes from addition, *per via di porre,* is similar to painting. But enough. As sculpture and painting both spring from the same mind, peace can be made between them, and all these discussions can be set aside, for they use up more time than the making of figures. Whoever wrote that painting is nobler than sculpture—if he is as learned about the other things he has written about—my servant could have written better about them than he does" (a remark directed probably against Leonardo). In spite of this, he says in the same letter: "I must say that to me painting seems better when it tends toward relief, and relief worse when it tends toward painting. Therefore I think in general that sculpture is the lamp of painting, and that the same difference exists between the two as between the sun and the moon." [15]

Although he retained his preference for sculpture, nevertheless he regarded the two artistic branches as equal. And it might be added that he also recognized no essential difference between these arts and architecture. In his opinion architecture was anthropomorphic. He says (Milanesi, p. 554): "È cosa certa, che le membra dell' architettura dipendono dalle membra dell' uomo." (It is certain that architectural members depend on the same rules as those governing the limbs of men.) This theory goes back to antiquity. It is found already in Vitruvius (*De Architectura,* Book III, ed. Krohn, p. 59). In the Renaissance the idea was revived by Filarete and L. B. Alberti; but these authors speak only of a "proportional correspondence" (*commensus responsum*) between the architectural members and the proportions of the human body, while Michelangelo speaks of dependence. We find this heightened anthropomorphic conception already anticipated in Fra Luca Pacioli, who had taken it from Leonardo. Pacioli speaks in his *Divina Proportione* (ed. Winterberg, p. 138) of the "derivation," the *derivazione* of the architectural members from those of the human body.

But it should be noticed that even with regard to these views Michelangelo's ideas underwent a change: in his youth he regarded himself as a sculptor in marble and signed his letters "Michelagniolo scultore." He would explain that painting, sculpture in bronze, and architecture were not his profession. Only after the completion of the Sistine Ceiling did he cease to put sculpture before painting and henceforth sign his letters simply: Michelagniolo.

Not until the last period of his life did he become the universal artist, who saw the three fine arts as equal in value because they spring from the same spirit.

Even in his first works, in the *Virgin of the Steps* and the *Battle of the Centaurs*, Michelangelo was translating an inner vision of beauty in marble and discarding all accidental beauty. His development did not consist in an advance from naturalism to idealism, but rather in the fact that the somewhat veiled inner image (*Virgin of the Steps, Battle of the Centaurs*), still indistinct at the beginning, became ever more concrete through the inclusion of realistic details (*David*), until the artist finally reached a harmonious balance of the two tendencies (Medici Chapel). At the end of his life, however, he came back in his religious works, with conscious intention, to the vague inner image which now again, as at the beginning, reflected in its dim, blurred outlines only the bare essentials.

Since Michelangelo never regarded the exact imitation of empirical nature as the purpose of art, he could not approve of the Flemish, Spanish, or German schools, or even of the Italian Quattrocento.[16]

Leonardo demands that the painter be universal, that he know not only man but all aspects of nature. Besides linear perspective, he must also study aerial perspective. He must know how to manage the values (*valeurs*) of colors—that is, their light content.[17] Michelangelo, however, regards man as the chief subject of art. Instead of the extensive universalism of the second half of the fifteenth century, he looks for a uni-

(92)

versalism in depth: the whole cosmos must be related to man and contained in him. This is why Michelangelo rejects the extensive and descriptive realistic painting of the early Netherlanders. Francisco de Hollanda reports that the master made these observations on the subject: "In Flanders they paint to stab the outer eye with things that please . . . they also paint draperies, tracery, green fields, shady trees, rivers, bridges, and what they call landscapes, as well as many figures in motion. . . . And although all this is pleasing to some eyes, nevertheless in truth real art is lacking, that is, proper proportion and proper scale, as well as the selection and clear division of space and finally the nerve and substance . . ." [18] In other words the Netherlanders paint nature without its laws, without showing its *idea*, that is to say without that beauty which alone deserves to be painted.

Nor was Michelangelo at all interested in individual features, that is, in painting portraits. He looked for the Idea of man.[19] In the Medici tombs he idealized the features of the Dukes in a way that struck even his contemporaries. Niccolò Martelli wrote to Rugasso in 1544: "Michelangelo . . . nella libreria di S. Lorenzo, havendo . . . a scolpire i Signori illustri della felicissima casa de' Medici, non tolse dal Duca Lorenzo, nè dal Sig. Giuliano il modello apunto come la natura gli avea effigiati e composti, ma diede loro una grandezza, une proportione, un decoro, una gratia, uno splendore qual gli parea che più lodi loro arrecassero, dicendo che di qui a mille anni nessuno non ne potea dar cognitione che fossero altrimenti . . ." [20] (When Michelangelo had to model the illustrious lords of the most worthy house of Medici in the library of San Lorenzo, he represented neither Duke Lorenzo nor Lord Giuliano exactly as nature had created them, but gave them the size, proportion, decorum, grace, and splendor that, in his opinion, would yield them most praise, for, as he said, a thousand years from then no one would know that

(93)

PLATE XXV

they had been otherwise . . .). He made portraits only as an exception, for instance the lost portrait of his friend Cavalieri and the portraits of the two sons of his *garzone* Urbino. We know from his poems that Cavalieri's face had for him a reflection of divine beauty. So it was no realistic portrait but —as indeed contemporary descriptions tell us—an idealized likeness.

Condivi, alluding to the *Venus of Croton* by Zeuxis, describes Michelangelo's method of work as one of selecting the most beautiful parts of several models and uniting them in one figure, thus making what was called the "ideal imitation" in treatises of the time.[21] Indeed, in a youthful poem (Frey, *Dicht.* IV) Michelangelo himself describes this selective method as the one used by God to create the world. Nevertheless this is not what happened in his own works. He never produced a mere compilation of the most beautiful parts of different models, but rather portrayed a unified vision of beauty. He adhered to his principle that a preoccupation with visible beauty awakens the memory to divine beauty; the first is a reflection of the divine light in the material (Frey, *Dicht.* XXXI). Michelangelo expressed this Platonic theory in his poetry more than once, especially during his relationship with Cavalieri. If he felt himself at certain moments struck by the beauty of his friend, he nevertheless saw in this beauty only the symbol of that divine beauty which elevates the soul to contemplate God (Frey, *Dicht.* LXIV; LXXIX; XCI; XCII; CIX, 66; CIX, 99; CIX, 101). Michelangelo's conception makes earthly beauty awaken in the soul an inner image, the "heart's image," which is superior to the material image (Frey, *Dicht.* XXXIV; LXII), and this "image in the heart" (*imagine del cor*) the artist incorporates into his material.

The inner image, *l'imagine del cor*, is naturally superior to the finished work, which is only a copy of it. The complete execution of a work of art, materially speaking, is therefore not absolutely indispensable. The incomplete can also possess a positive value, for it communicates the whole inner image even though it is itself fragmentary. Furthermore, an unfinished work can often reproduce the inner image even more faithfully through its indefinite spiritual character, which is confined to the essential. Vasari and Condivi point this out to us. Referring to the *Medici Virgin*, Vasari (1550) says: "Ancora che non siano finite le parti sue, si conosce nell' essere rimasta abozzata e gradinata nella imperfettione della bozza, la perfettione dell' opera." (One can recognize the perfection of the work, even though its parts are incomplete, in the imperfect tooth-chiseling of the rough-hewn block.) Vasari clearly differentiates here between the perfection of the inner spiritual image and its imperfect material realization. Shortly after this, Condivi expanded Vasari's judgment of the unfinished, applying it to the whole Medici Chapel: "lo sbozzo non impedisce la perfezione e la bellezza del opera" (the roughhewn marble does not prevent the work from being perfect and beautiful).[22]

Michelangelo's unfinished work has often been explained as being due to the fact that the artist was prevented by unfavorable external circumstances from completing it, or that he was dissatisfied with himself. Most modern critics attribute the unfinished character of the works to the impossibility of Michelangelo's being able to put his gigantic plans into practice. But the "unfinished" has also been explained as an artistic necessity.[23] This argument suggests that Michelangelo must certainly have regarded his incomplete statues as unfinished works, because his artistic ideal was founded on the power of the *rilievo*. He did not complete his statues, in spite of this, because in so doing he would have lessened their lyric intensity. Still, Vasari's contemporary account seems to show that Michelangelo did not regard his unfinished figures as incomplete, but as full realizations of the "inner image."

PLATE XV

Even his two earliest reliefs he left unfinished, and in the *Battle of the Centaurs*[24] his intention seems to have been to bring out more impressively the softness of the human bodies in contrast to the roughhewn block which surrounds them like a frame. There results from this treatment a difference in color, the more completed parts appearing lighter than the roughhewn parts. Michelangelo seems to have used this device consciously at different periods of his life up till his last works. The body of the Christ (except for the face) in the late *Deposition* in the Cathedral of Florence is completely finished and even polished. However, it is framed by the roughhewn figures of Joseph of Arimathea and the Virgin. Originally Mary Magdalene was also roughhewn, but was later finished by Michelangelo's pupil Tiberio Calcagni. But even in the figures which are finished this principle of contrasting the smooth and rough parts is present, since the drapery now assumes the artistic function of the roughhewn parts (*Pietà*, St. Peter's; *Moses*, San Pietro in Vincoli).

Matter in itself is lifeless; it is the artist who causes life to flow into the marble by drawing out of it the potential idea slumbering there (Frey, *Dicht.* LXV). The inner image, *l'imagine del cor*, in the artist's soul, and the image that he sees within the rough block are identical, for both are nothing other than the Idea.

The method of creation by which a plastic work results from the removal of what is superfluous in the material "per forza di levare" goes back to Aristotle (*Metaphysics,* IX, 6), and received an ethical interpretation from Plotinus and the ancient Neo-Platonists. To them pure form freeing itself from the dull mass of the stone was a symbol of catharsis and the soul's rebirth (Plotinus, *Enneads,* I, 6–9).[25] This thought lived on in the Middle Ages with Dionysius Areopagita and Thomas Aquinas. The theorists of art in the early Renaissance revived it and made a simple workshop recipe out of it,

(96)

without taking over its ethical symbolism as well. We find it in this form in L. B. Alberti, Leonardo, and Vasari.

It has been observed that only Michelangelo, in adopting this theory, returned to it its ethical meaning (Panofsky). Pure form released from matter was the symbol of rebirth for him, too, although he did not experience it, like Plotinus, as an auto-cartharsis, but as a purification achieved through the Beloved Woman—Vittoria Colonna (Frey, *Dicht.* LXXXIV and CXXXIV).

Just as the potentiality of beautiful or ugly works lies hidden in a block of marble, and just as the form which is freed from the marble depends on the artist's mind (*l'ingegno*) (Frey, *Dicht.* LXV), in the same way the potentiality for good and evil lies in the beloved being, and it depends on the lover, the *amatore*, which alternative he wins.

In a very real way the primitive form of the block had a decisive influence on Michelangelo's imagination (Frey, *Dicht.* LXXXIII). As he became absorbed in it, the inner image awoke in him; one can actually see how in his sculptures and reliefs he always allowed himself to be guided by the primitive form of the block, and in his frescoes by the dimension and shape of the surfaces at his disposal. It was the true form and mass of the vault of the Sistine Chapel that inspired Michelangelo, and in this he was the opposite of his predecessors who had taken pains to cover the true form and weight of the vault by painting the vault over with a decorative system which does not interpret the structure. They concealed the construction either through a network of cornices and fields or by illusionist painting.[26] Michelangelo took possession of the curved surface of the ceiling just as it was offered to him, and brought out of it a world of gigantic figures and an architectural structure which exposed the vital forces immanent in it. He translated the material weight of the ceiling into his gigantic figures of seers and into the "relief" of the painted architectural trellis. He expressed symbolically the thrusting forces latent in the ceiling by means of broad elastic bands, the tension of which is personified also by the caryatid-*putti* replacing the capitals of the pillars. The binding force, which counteracts the side-thrust, he symbolized by a powerfully profiled entablature which projects around the pillars and links the whole system together. Michelangelo even found the plastic symbol that explains on an artistic level the curve of the whole ceiling; he interpreted it as a consequence of the weight of the Sibyls and Prophets, whose heavy mass pulls the giant framework downward. So the whole system brings the latent energies of the ceiling into play. It seems to be curved by its own weight and held up by its own tension. It is an autonomous and sovereign world.

When he painted the *Last Judgment*, Michelangelo was inspired in the same way by the material circumstances of the altar wall of the Sistine Chapel, regarding it as a monolith. The division of the groups of figures into zones on the surface of the wall is explained by the structure of the chapel itself; the height of the groups is more or less decided by the height of the cornices of the side walls, and the central axis originates in the Quattrocento console.[27] The composition is arranged around this axis according to the laws of symmetry and *contrapposto*. The groups on each side correspond and at the same time contrast in movement with each other, just as each part of the human body has its counterpart (cf. Michelangelo's letter, Milanesi, p. 554). Each significant figure of the fresco has its counterpart on the other side. This world of human figures does not seem to be painted on the wall; rather, it seems to have slumbered in the wall until the artist awakened it. The entire composition is in itself an organic body.

In his reliefs, too, Michelangelo was guided by the material realities of the stone. He constantly retained the edges of

PLATE XXXV

the block in his works, showing the primitive form and thickness. He penetrated the surface in parallel planes according to the crystalline structure of the stone. In the *Battle of the Centaurs* he left the roughhewn stone behind the figures, so that even those limbs which stand out most strongly still remain joined to the material. Here too, the single figures seem not to be applied to the relief ground but to be born of the homogeneous mass of the stone.

Michelangelo adopted the same principle for his sculptures in the round. Again he retained in the finished statue the primitive outline of the stone block, which is repeated in the silhouette of the statue. The base reveals the original proportions of the block. Even the gestures of the figures are determined in a way by the block, and nothing protrudes beyond this strictly circumscribed "block" space.[28] In this he goes back directly to the methods of the great sculptors of the cathedrals of the thirteenth and fourteenth centuries. But in the column-statues of the Middle Ages the forms and movements of the figures are completely controlled by the shape of the block to which they are passively subordinated; Michelangelo's figures, however, seem to rebel against this constriction which nevertheless confines them. What Michelangelo actually did was to attack the block directly and to draw the figure out of it. Mostly he worked from the front toward the back, penetrating layer by layer into the block as if he were making a "series of reliefs." He finished single parts of the figure—and often left them surrounded by roughly hewn marble. Sometimes he started at the corner of the block, penetrating diagonally into it—this he did when the figure was to be placed at the corner of a monument.

Such a method of working leaves the planes either parallel or perpendicular to the surface of the block; the front and back planes are always parallel to the primary surface of the block, and these two levels are sometimes linked by a short

(99)

PLATE II

connecting diagonal. The reclining figures in the Medici Chapel are also conceived on this principle.

The large plastic compositions with numerous figures, such as the Tomb of Julius II, the Sistine Ceiling, and the Medici tombs, are conceived according to this method of parallel planes as if they were hewn out of a gigantic monolith. That is why they do not give the impression of an array of statues like similar compositions in the Middle Ages, for instance Nicola and Giovanni Pisano's pulpits, but rather of a homogeneous whole, which seems to have been differentiated a posteriori. The relationship between the architectural framework and the plastic figures in these three cyclic works is also newly defined. Whereas in the Middle Ages the lines of the architecture always determine the location and the form of the figures, Michelangelo gradually freed his figures from this tradition, attaining in the Medici tombs an emancipation of the figural composition in front of the architecture. This resulted in the effect of two systems, figural and architectural, which together created a new unity, and the simple melody of the earlier device is replaced by a rich and powerful symphony.

After Michelangelo finally settled in Rome in 1534, he first renounced the representation of physical beauty and later even that of physical strength. The first change is manifest in the *Last Judgment*, the second in the last works. His late poems also proclaim that "bodily beauty passes": love of this beauty is madness, and can never bring satisfaction (Frey, *Dicht.* CIX, 34).

The religious images of Michelangelo's last creative period look almost transparent, as if they were illuminated by a diffused inner light; they seem to emanate a soft aura which at once surrounds them and isolates them. By means of this

PLATES XXIX, XXX, XXXIII, XXXIV, XLIV TO XLVI

phosphorescence, the artist imparts to his works the luminosity characteristic of mystic visions. The bodies of the figures lose their corporeal aspect. They are transparent, simplified in their outlines; the power with which they once pulsated becomes extinguished. These may be called purely spiritual realities. The forms emerge from the paper like apparitions, quite independent of any conception of real space. Perhaps such an effect is the result of precisely this process of creating inner images: the spiritual concentration which brings them forth cannot at once call into being the countless elements needed to form a complete world. They appear in a vacuum, in unlimited space. The distinctness of the forms dissolves at the periphery into the undetermined.

Two sculptures which Michelangelo did during the last twenty years of his life indicate that he tried to convey the same immaterial visions in marble too. The surface of the *Deposition* (Florence, Cathedral) reveals a mixture of smooth and rough working of the marble. On the rough surfaces the light is broken and diffuse, and this somehow gives the heads of Joseph of Arimathea and the Virgin that transparent character which we have already noticed in the master's last drawings.[29]

Again, in the *Pietà* formerly in the Rondanini Palace (now in Castello Sforzesco, Milan) the artist subordinated bodily strength and beauty to the power of spiritual radiance. The external appearance of both figures seems to be bare of all physical strength and beauty. The group's silhouette is angular and straight, its surface shows—except for the polished parts done for the first version—the rough technique which Michelangelo used to soften the strong contrast between light and shade, and with which he achieved the half-tones which at the same time serve to bring out the inner light.

It seems obvious therefore that Michelangelo came quite consciously to the use of rough surfaces; the master found it

(101)

PLATES XX, XXI

an appropriate means to express the spiritualization of his figures and their inner radiance.

Francisco de Hollanda has Michelangelo say in his *Dialogue:* "In order to copy the image of our Lord, it is not enough to be a good, skillful painter; I think one must also lead a blameless life, as holy a life as possible, so that the Holy Ghost inspires one to understand Jesus Christ." Valdés in his *Considerazioni* says the same thing, and this thought had already been expressed in similar words by Savonarola. It seems to be the key to an understanding of Michelangelo's last works, which truly were created "under the inspiration of the Holy Ghost." Michelangelo now puts aside all his knowledge of the human body, all his learning about art, and goes back to creating his inner images in a naïve and direct way, obeying only the dictates of his soul. His last works are also no longer what the earlier ones were: incarnations of archetypes. They now assume a purely personal significance: they must help Michelangelo to justify his soul. He communicates to them what he needs most: divine love. Indeed, his two last sculptures were not commissioned but were made for himself alone.

The general principles of Michelangelo's artistic credo, as we have tried to outline it, are differentiated by him according to the content of the subject he is handling.

The early works of political content (*David, Battle of Cascina*) are treated with a scientific realism which does not occur in either the religious or philosophical works of the same period.

The works of philosophic content, incorporating the anthropocentric ideals of humanism, are presented in an architectural framework whose function is to make the human form stand out distinctly and take its proper place (Tomb of

PLATES VIII, V

Julius II and Sistine Ceiling). The works of cosmological content of the late Roman period (*Last Judgment* and frescoes of the Pauline Chapel), on the contrary, present the figures as subordinate to a rotating movement in unlimited space. Their movements and positions are determined by the magnetic powers of attraction which control them. One might add that in the period which has been termed here the most humanistic and anthropocentric, the figures achieve a complete physiological expansion in the sense of the ancient ideal of beauty, whereas in his cosmological period Michelangelo renounces bodily beauty and conceives the human form as a massive block.

The religious experience in the "antique" sense, which actuated the artist in his youth, is expressed in a classical idiom based on antiquity. The religious spirit of the Old Testament is interpreted under the influence of the late Gothic but at the same time "protobaroque" works of Quercia, which are so rich in movement. The works of the last period, which stemmed from his Christian experience (the Pietà groups) have sometimes, with their pointed forms and accentuation of the vertical, something of a Gothic character.[30]

So Michelangelo expresses himself in different artistic languages each determined partly by the content of the work. However, these languages are not always clearly differentiated, especially in the early works. Nevertheless the *Doni Virgin,* a seemingly religious theme, anticipates the Sistine Ceiling in its style and thus stands in contrast to the nearly contemporary and integrally religious *Virgin of Bruges.* A closer look at the *Doni Virgin* reveals that Michelangelo is not essentially concerned with its religious theme, but rather with its philosophical connotation (cf. Chapter II), so its style conforms to its inner content.

By the parallel use of these different artistic languages Michelangelo put into practice one of the main principles of

(103)

PLATES XXX, XXXV TO XXXVII, XX, XXI, V, III

his aesthetic theory: namely, that the form of a work of art must conform to its purpose.

The development of Michelangelo's political convictions from the patriotism of the Florentine citizen to the ideals of the world citizen of Christianity; the unfolding of his philosophy, which began as anthropocentric humanism and ended in a cosmological vision; the expansion of his religious beliefs from the *fatum* concepts of the ancients into an evangelical love; the spiritualization of his art from the archetype of beauty into a mystic vision of divine love: these stages were only different aspects of the development of the indivisible unity of his ethical personality.

Michelangelo regarded himself as one of those marble blocks from Carrara whose inherent idea he wanted to liberate—first through the medium of the Beloved Woman, later with the help of the Savior. He worked unceasingly at his own perfection. Bold of spirit, proud and of unruly temperament in his youth, he became first a contemplative thinker (period of the Medici Chapel) by renouncing these inborn characteristics, and then a humble Christian (final period). As a young man he epitomized the flowering of the Florentine genius in its perfection. At the end of his life he grew beyond it and achieved a Christian universalism. The ruling force of his personality was "l'ardente desio," the ardent yearning toward the higher spheres, toward "ideas." "Al ciel sempre son mosso . . . ," "Al cielo aspiro . . . ," he says in his poems. This metaphysical nostalgia revealed itself in different ways: first as Platonism, then as Christianity. The master incorporated it directly into several of his drawings with both pagan and Christian subjects, as well as in his other works. For instance, he used the fable of Ganymede as a symbol of this ascension of the soul. He makes a closely knit group out of the eagle and the figure of Ganymede.[31] On the eagle he bestows an expression of human suffering. The bird eagerly

PLATE XLI

seizes the tender young body in its talons and encircles it with outstretched neck. The boy, unresisting, allows the abduction to take place, and seems to be sunk in an erotic dream. From a distance the pair seem to be a single winged being, an expression of that mystic union of love of which Michelangelo speaks in his poems to Cavalieri, for whom the drawing was actually done as a gift:

> *Un' anima in due corpi è fatta eterna,*
> *Ambo levando al cielo e con pari ale . . .*
>
> (Frey, *Dicht.* XLIV)

> (A single soul in two bodies becomes eternal,
> Both rising to heaven on the same wings.)

Again, in three drawings representing Christ's Resurrection, which belong to the years between 1525 and 1531, Michelangelo symbolizes the purely spiritual urgings of the soul, as it frees itself from earthly bonds (*carcer terreno*). Traditionally Christ is portrayed in Resurrection images as the conqueror of death, stepping from the tomb with a banner in his hand, one foot still in the sarcophagus and the other resting on its rim. Michelangelo, in his red chalk sketch in Paris, dramatizes this scene in another way: Christ, a naked, beardless, Apollonian figure, is bursting from the tomb with a stormy movement, as if inwardly seized at the call of liberation. In his yearning for freedom and light he seems to be passionately striving toward the divine. The dramatic effect is further strengthened by the contrast between his body, drawn diagonally on the sheet, and the confused mass of the startled soldiers who stagger back.

The Christ in the second version, in Windsor, is almost the same one, but the twisting of his body is less pronounced and this makes his straining toward the heights all the more impressive. The watch are more numerous; they are huddled together as if in heavy sleep after an orgy, and from this at-

(105)

PLATE XXXIX

mosphere of drunkenness (drunkenness is—as we have already noted—in the Platonic sense the symbol of the soul's imprisonment in the body) the powerful, supple body of Christ rises in a vigorous movement. He is at once the symbol of the soul's spiritual ascension to the light and the expression of Michelangelo's own longings.

The third drawing, in London, shows the slender body of the still-sleeping Christ being borne gently into the air. This apparition drives the crowd of soldiers to the outskirts— as light drives out darkness. It is the transformation of man into a heavenly spirit which dazzles the earthbound.[32]

In his early youth Michelangelo still belonged to the type of craftsman artificer represented by the artists of the fifteenth century and he proudly signed his letters "Michelagniolo scultore." Later, however, he regarded himself as belonging to a higher social order and in his old age he even protested against being called "scultore." "I have never been a painter or a sculptor as such with a shop [on the market place]; for the honor of my father and my brothers I have always guarded against that . . ."[33]

But on the other hand, he was not yet an artist-aristocrat living a splendid, worldly life in his palace and having his projects carried out by his pupils, as did some artists of the sixteenth and seventeenth centuries (Raphael, Zuccari, Bernini, Rubens, Van Dyck, and others). Michelangelo always executed his works himself.

In his maturity he was much more the type of artist-philosopher and artist-poet, an aristocrat of the spirit. Leonardo's recommendations (*Trattato*, par. 63) to the artist: that he "live in solitude, in order to concentrate better on the essence of things," Michelangelo carried out in full measure throughout his life.

PLATE XL

There is a surprising contrast between the sublime world of his creations and his actual life. In his life he was an anguished, suspicious, melancholy man, difficult to handle, at once timid and proud, in whose existence we can find hardly any reflection of that heroic world which he engendered in his spirit. He seems to have compensated for the inadequacies and shortcomings of his physical being, from which he suffered deeply, only through the supernatural beings in his works.

From the very beginning Michelangelo sought in his art the Idea which in nature shines through the visible form. His conception of art led to a new conception of the artist. He was no longer a mere imitator of nature but a second creator, a quasi-deity, who in his works surpassed visible nature in order to lay bare the "true nature."

In his *Trattato della Pittura* (about 1435, Book III) Leone Battista Alberti warns the artist—in the middle of the Quattrocento—against placing too much trust in his genius, and advises him to confine himself to the great model that is nature. He should not follow the example of those wrongheaded fools who, proud of their talent, hope to win praise and glory for their painting without using an existing prototype. He says: "Ma per non perdere studio et faticha, si vuole fuggire quella consuetudine d'alcuni sciocchi, i quali presuntuosi di suo ingegnio, senza avere essemplo alcuno dalla natura, quale con occhi o mente seguano, studiano da se ad se acquistare lode di dipigniere. Questi non imparano dipigniere bene, ma assuefanno se a suoi errori. Fuggie l'ingegni non periti quella idea delle bellezze, quali i beni exercitatissimi appena discernono."

Toward the turn of the century Leonardo da Vinci had already gone beyond this conception, which subordinated creative genius to empirical nature. He postulated a balance between nature and creative genius. The artistic fantasy wants to grasp the inner laws of nature. The artist does not invent; he finds and reveals in his works the hidden laws of nature. He does not imitate nature exclusively but creates according to the creative principles revealed to human reason by nature.[34]

Michelangelo went beyond even this conception: no longer an empiricist but a Platonist, he argued that the artistic fantasy must recreate "true reality," the world of ideas, of which visible nature is but a weak reflection. The creative artist is a true Prometheus, his spirit is an image of God's spirit. He is superior to visible nature, for he is himself the creator of a second reality superior to the first. This proud conception of the artist was, however, abandoned and revoked by Michelangelo in his last years, when he became a Christian. Then he no longer created in his works a world of archetypes but a vision of the divine. But even there he never renounced the creation of another transcendent reality.

NOTES

Bibliographical Abbreviations

Condivi   Ascanio Condivi, *Vita di Michelangelo Buo-*
                 narroti (1553). References are to *Le Vite di*
                 Michelangelo Buonarroti scritte da Giorgio
                 Vasari e da Ascanio Condivi, ed. Carl Frey
                 (Berlin, 1887).

Frey, *Dicht.*   Carl Frey, *Die Dichtungen des Michelagniolo*
                 Buonarroti (Berlin, 1897).

Milanesi   Gaetano Milanesi, *Le Lettere di Michelangelo*
                 Buonarroti (Florence, 1875).

Tolnay I   Charles de Tolnay, *The Youth of Michelan-*
                 gelo, 2nd ed. (Princeton, 1947).

Tolnay II   *Idem, The Sistine Ceiling,* 2nd ed.
                 (Princeton, 1949).

Tolnay III   *Idem, The Medici Chapel* (Princeton, 1948).

Tolnay IV   *Idem, The Tomb of Julius II* (Princeton,
                 1954).

Tolnay V   *Idem, The Final Period* (Princeton, 1960).

Vasari,   Giorgio Vasari, *Vite de' Più Eccelenti Pittori,*
  1550 and   *Scultori, ed Architetti Italiani* (1550; 2nd ed.
  1568   1568). References are to *Le Vite di Michel-*
                 angelo Buonarroti scritte da Giorgio Vasari
                 e da Ascanio Condivi, ed. Carl Frey (Berlin,
                 1887).

CHAPTER I

1. Cf. G. B. Niccolini, *Del Sublime e di Michelagniolo*
    (Florence, 1825).

    F. D. Guerrazzi, *L'Assedio di Firenze* (Romanzo
    Storico) (Paris, 1836). Cf. on this novel: G. Fucini,

"Michelangelo e l'Assedio di Firenze di Guerrazzi," in *Rivista Liburni Civitas,* III (1930).

M. Missirini, *Difesa di Michelagniolo Buonarroti per la sua partenza da Firenze* (Florence, 1840).

2. G. Gaye, "Sulla Fuga di Michelagniolo da Firenze nel 1529," in *Rivista Europea,* III (June, 1839), pp. 107 ff.

Idem: Carteggio inedito d'artisti dei secoli XIV, XV, XVI, Vol. II (Florence, 1840), pp. 213 ff.

C. Milanesi, "Condotta di Michelagniolo Buonarroti, Soprintendente delle fortificazioni di Firenze," in *Giornale Storico degli Archivi Toscani* (Florence, 1858), pp. 66 f.; cf. also *Il Vasari,* III, pp. 366 f.

Lettere di G. B. Busini a Varchi sopra l'Assedio di Firenze, ed. G. Milanesi (Florence, 1860).

I. del Lungo, in *Archivio Storico Italiano,* Ser. III (Florence, 1865), I (2), pp. 156 ff.

G. Guerzoni, "Michelangelo Cittadino. La politica nel Cinquecento," in *Nuova Antologia,* XXI (Florence, 1872), pp. 513 ff. and 780 ff. After a general introduction to Italian politics in the sixteenth century the author concerns himself only with the episode of Michelangelo's flight in 1529.

3. "Abbiamo pagato trecento anni le gravezze a Firenze" (Milanesi, p. 436).

4. "Noi siamo pure cittadini discesi di nobilissima stirpe" (Milanesi, p. 197) (Yet we are citizens descended from a noble line); "Siamo antichi cittadini fiorentini e nobili quant' e ogni altra casa" (Milanesi, p. 237; cf. also Milanesi, pp. 271 and 492) (We are old Florentine citizens, and our house is as noble as any other).

5. G. Poggi, "Note Michelagniolesche: Michelangelo e il Machiavelli," in *Michelagniolo Buonarroti nel IV Centenario del Giudizio Universale* (Florence, 1942), pp. 129 ff.

6. M. Augustin Renaudet deals with this point of view in his *Machiavel* (Paris, 1942).

    Cf. also the excellent book by R. Ridolfi, *Vita di Niccolò Machiavelli* (Rome, 1954).

7. Cf. the two sonnets dedicated to Dante by Michelangelo, cf. Frey, *Dicht.* CIX, 37: "il nido, ove nacqu'io"; Frey, *Dicht.* CIX, 49: "nutrice." There is an excellent new critical edition of Michelangelo's poems by E. N. Girardi, *Michelagniolo Buonarroti, Rime* (Bari, 1960). There are two recent new translations of the poems into English: one by Joseph Tusiani (New York, 1960), another by Creighton Gilbert (New York, 1963). Neither of these translations succeeds completely in rendering the flavor of the originals.

    In the *Esequie del Divino Michelagniolo* (Florence, 1564; here quoted after the edition of 1875, p. 23), it is stated that he was always "tenerissimo amatore" of "Fiorenza, sua nobilissima patria."

    In a book recently published in the U.S.A., Michelangelo's Florentine patriotism is called an "extremely nationalistic bias." It seems to me that this interpretation is based on a profound misunderstanding of the master's spirit.

8. In the *Esequie,* p. 23, we read that several times he asked Lionardo Buonarroti and Daniele da Volterra "che il suo corpo fusse portato a Firenze."

9. As almost the entire correspondence for the years 1496–1501 is lost, we have only a single direct account (1497, Milanesi, p. 4) of Michelangelo's homesickness during his first stay in Rome; but we possess similar information concerning his stay in Bologna in 1507 (Letter from Bologna, Milanesi, p. 84) and in Venice in 1529 (Letter from Venice, Milanesi, p. 457).

10. The Operai di Santa Maria del Fiore and the Consoli

dell'Arte della Lana handed over to him a marble block, from which he was to create a David; the Consoli dell'Arte della Lana commissioned him to make the twelve Apostles for the Cathedral of Florence; the Signoria, i.e. the Gonfaloniere Piero Soderini, ordered a bronze David from him and a large fresco for the "Sala del gran Consiglio" in the Palazzo della Signoria, the subject of which was to be the Battle of Cascina.

11. For the history of the *David*, cf. Tolnay I, pp. 93 ff. and 150 ff.

12. Cf. Tolnay, "Two frescoes by Domenico and David Ghirlandaio in Santa Trinità in Florence," in *Wallraf-Richartz Jahrbuch* (Cologne, 1961), pp. 237 ff.

13. Tolnay I, p. 94.

The seventeen-year-old Michelangelo executed, without commission, after the death of Lorenzo de' Medici (in April 1492) an over-life-sized (four *braccia*, or nearly 233 cm., high) marble figure of Hercules. His intention was to attract the Florentines to his *bravura* and thereby to find a new Maecenas. He chose Hercules as subject probably because this ancient hero was considered a patron of Florence. The figure is briefly described by Vasari, p. 29, and Condivi, p. 28. It came into possession of the Strozzi family, but was, in 1529, acquired for the collections of Francis I. Henry IV later (ca. 1594) erected the statue on a richly decorated base in the center of the Jardin de l'Estang of Fontainebleau. In 1713, this garden was destroyed and since that time, the statue has been lost. An etching by Israel Silvestre, reproducing the Jardin de l'Estang with the figure in its center, seen from the back, was discovered by Tolnay and published in the *Jahrbuch der preussischen Kunstsammlungen* (1933). A hitherto unnoticed frontal view of the figure is preserved in a Rubens drawing (Louvre),

(114)

PLATE VII

which permits us to define for the first time the importance of this lost early work for Michelangelo's development. It shows the *contrapposto* motif, in a reversed version, of the marble *David*. The position of the legs is already inspired by ancient Hercules figures; the lion skin sits on the back of the head and falls behind onto the back, like the draperies of Donatello's early *David* and *St. George* (this motif is clearly visible in Israel Silvestre's etching). Thus the figure directly anticipated the marble *David* of about nine years later, which therefore appears to us now as less of a surprise.

The red wax model of a naked youth in the Casa Buonarroti, which up to now has always been connected with the marble *David*, should be considered as the original *modello* for the Hercules, since its *contrapposto* is identical. The right arm of this *modello*, which originally probably held the club, was already broken off around the middle of the sixteenth century, as is attested to by two drawings of this *modello* in the Uffizi. In two small bronze copies of the later sixteenth century, this arm has been erroneously reconstructed to look like the raised arm of the marble *David*. The statuette was already so celebrated in the sixteenth century that it figures as an emblem in one of the Michelangelo portraits in the Casa Buonarroti. Mention may be made that in the Guardaroba of Duke Cosimo I (1553–68) the *modello* is described as "uno modello di stucco del Gigante di Michelagniolo" (Steinmann-Wittkower, *Michelangelo Bibliographie* [Leipzig, 1927], p. 432). It is not clear whether "Gigante" means here Hercules or David, since it could be either one.

An example of the ancient Hercules type which inspired Michelangelo is Clarac, No. 1996 (cf. S. Reinach, *Repertoire de la statuaire grecque et romaine* (Paris,

1920), Vol. I, p. 470). The position of the legs, the motif of the lion skin falling from the head down the back, are taken from such an example; the club, however, does not touch the ground in the ancient figure. (We intend to treat our discovery in more detail on a later occasion.)

14. May I refer the reader at this point to the important works of H. Baron, who deals with the theories of *fortezza* and *ira* in the writings of the Florentine humanists of the early fifteenth century; our text uses the results of his investigations. Baron does not mention Michelangelo's *David* in this connection, however.

Cf. H. Baron, "La Rinascità dell' Etica statale Romana nell' Umanesimo Fiorentino," in *Civiltà Moderna*, VII (1935), pp. 3 ff.; *idem:* "Cicero and the Roman Civic Spirit in the Middle Ages and Early Renaissance," in *Bulletin of the John Rylands Library, Manchester*, XXII (1938), pp. 72 ff.; *idem: The Crisis of the Italian Renaissance* (Princeton, 1955); *idem: Humanistic and Political Literature in Florence and Venice at the Beginning of the Quattrocento* (Cambridge, Mass., 1955).

15. Cf. H. Baron, works cited in preceding note.

16. The Commission's report gives us an instructive glimpse of the different, partly traditional, partly progressive opinions then circulating in Florence. Two points of view can be inferred from them: one bound by tradition, represented by those who wished to preserve the religious character of this work and therefore to place it in the vicinity of the cathedral; another, more progressive-minded group wanted to secularize the statue and to place it either in the Loggia dei Lanzi or near the Palazzo della Signoria. The arguments advanced in favor of these different *pareri* were for either practical or artistic reasons. For instance it was maintained that the

statue would be more sheltered in the Loggia dei Lanzi, where it would not be exposed to the ravages of the seasons, or else it was contended that it would be better admired in front of the Palazzo. A carpenter, Francesco Monciatto, was the only one in favor of respecting the original wishes of the Operai del Duomo. He suggested placing the statue on one of the buttresses of the choir of the cathedral, for which the block had originally been destined. Others at the meeting, and especially those artists belonging to an older generation than Michelangelo, likewise wanted to have the statue erected in the vicinity of the cathedral; they put forward the proposal that it should be set on a base to the right of the main portal of the cathedral, so that it could be better seen.

The majority of the *pareri* revealed themselves to be antitraditional and advocated removing the *David* from the vicinity of the cathedral and handing it over to the Signoria, so that it could be put in the Loggia dei Lanzi, where the great official festivities of the city were held. The main argument for this lay in the assertion that the work would be more protected in the Loggia. The second Herald of Florence emphasized as well that the statue would be honored there on account of the Palazzo ("honorata per conto del palazzo"); and since the Palazzo was regarded as a symbol of the Republic, this was already an identification of Michelangelo's work with the republican idea. Only a minority wanted to see the statue in the immediate confines of the Palazzo; and four different suggestions were made in this respect: the first that it should replace Donatello's *David* in the middle of the courtyard (two *pareri*); the second that it should be in the middle of the Sala del gran Consiglio (one *parere*); the third that it should replace Donatello's

Marzocco in front of the Palazzo (two *pareri*); and the last that it should be placed instead of Donatello's *Judith* on the parapet in front of the façade, to the left of the main entry and in the axis of the tower (one *parere*).

17. Michelangelo's *David* was placed in the axis of the tower of the Palazzo della Signoria. It is interesting to note that the same position in the axis of the tower of the Palazzo Pubblico in Siena was reserved for the Virgin. This shows that the site was considered to be an important one. But in more conservative Siena it was reserved for a religious purpose; in more modern Florence, for a political symbol.

18. Cf. Tolnay I, pp. 205 ff.

19. Cf. Tolnay III, pp. 98 ff.

20. Besides these sketches there still exists a terracotta model by Michelangelo in the Casa Buonarroti, which was probably intended for the same project. Cf. Tolnay III, pp. 98 ff.

21. Cf. Tolnay I, pp. 209 ff.

H. von Einem, *Michelangelo* (Stuttgart, 1959), pp. 33 ff.

For a reconstruction of the Sala del gran Consiglio as it was when Michelangelo was to execute his fresco there, cf. J. Wilde, *Journal of the Warburg and Courtauld Institutes* (1944); and *idem, The Burlington Magazine* (1953).

22. Cf. Tolnay III, pp. 10 ff.

23. Cf. Tolnay, *Art Bulletin*, XXII (1940), pp. 130 ff., and *idem, Michel-Ange* (Paris, 1951), illustrations 350 to 353. The series of drawings of fortifications is published in these works for the first time and analyzed from both the military and artistic points of view.

J. Ackerman, *The Architecture of Michelangelo*, Vol. II (London, 1961), pp. 43 ff., agrees with my opinions. Ackerman suggests the date 1528 for the drawings.

24. A. Gotti, *Vita di Michelangelo Buonarroti*, Vol. I (Florence, 1875), pp. 195 f.

25. Tolnay III, pp. 181 f.

26. From a letter of 1534 (Milanesi, p. 471) we know that Michelangelo had made the decision not to go back to Florence. (Later, however, in the fifties, he changed his mind.) Certainly Michelangelo could not have been impelled to make this decision because he was incensed by the ingratitude of the Florentines, even though he complained about the "popolo ingrato," as the Florentines gave him, unlike Dante, overt proof of their gratitude. In a series of letters the Medici Duke Cosimo I later invited Michelangelo with such gentle insistence ("con tanta dolcezza") to return that the artist was touched by it (Frey, *Dicht.*, p. 535; Milanesi, p. 534). At the duke's instigation Vasari urged him to come back in the following words: "Fly from the greedy Babylon and do as Petrarch did, who in the face of a like ingratitude chose the peace of Padua." And Varchi expresses the love and gratitude in which Florence held Michelangelo in these beautiful words: ". . . this whole city wishes in all humility to see you and to honor you at close hand as it does now from afar. Your Excellency would show great kindness by honoring your fatherland with your presence and causing it to rejoice therein; there you could live, after so many years away, in supreme liberty and tranquillity under a duke who is as good as he is just, as virtuous as he is great . . ." (Frey, *Dicht.*, p. 537). Michelangelo was fond of comparing his exile with the "aspro esilio," the very much sterner banishment, of Dante. He was moved by the unjust fate that the "ungrateful people" had inflicted on the greatest of its sons, when it closed to him the gates of his native

city, "whereas the gates of Paradise opened for him."
He was enraged that Florence, without having deserved
it, had become celebrated by the fame of the exile ra-
diating from abroad. In 1519 Michelangelo offered to
erect in Florence without fee a worthy monument to the
"divino poeta," in homage to the great exile and patriot.
The love and respect in which he held Dante were not
impaired by the fact that the latter was politically on the
other side, that he favored the restoration of the empire
and the reform of the Holy See. This is a further proof
that Michelangelo did not get involved in party politics
and that he subordinated everything else to his love for
the "nido ove nacqu'io." According to the *Esequie*
(1564), p. 23, "he was for many years absent (from
Florence) for no other reason than because of the
quality of the air. . . . Rome has conserved him in
excellent health until his ninetieth year." These climatic
reasons may also have played a role in his decisions, but
the reasons given by the artist himself seem to be more
important.

27. For the bust cf. Tolnay, "Michelangelo's Bust of Brutus,"
in *The Burlington Magazine*, LXVII (1935), pp. 23 ff.,
and Tolnay IV, pp. 76 ff. and 131 ff. The year 1546, suggested by Roberto Ridolfi, *Opuscoli di Storia Letteraria
e di Erudizione* (Florence, 1942), pp. 126 f., as the date
of the *Brutus*, is not likely because this bust is stylistically different from Michelangelo's other works (e.g.
Rachel and *Leah*) of that period.

28. *Dialoghi di Donato Giannotti*, ed. D. Redig de Campos
(Florence, 1939).

Cf. D. J. Gordon, *Festschrift Fritz Saxl* (London,
1957).

29. Cf. H. Tietze, "Francisco de Hollanda und Donato Gian-
nottis Dialoge und Michelangelo," in *Repertorium für*

Kunstwissenschaft, XXVIII (1905), pp. 295 ff. and R. J. Clements, *Michelangelo's Theory of Art* (New York, 1961). In my opinion only certain parts of Francisco de Hollanda's dialogues are reliable. The other parts are obviously written with the intention of influencing his patron.

30. In 1825 Niccolini (*op. cit.*) explained the Medici Chapel as the expression of Michelangelo's patriotic grief and saw in the statues of the Dukes the expression of his hatred of tyranny. This interpretation of Michelangelo's way of thinking may well be valid for the middle of the forties, that is, for that period of the artist's life when he was composing his poem on the *Notte,* but it is not so for the period during which he drew up his plans for the Chapel, a quarter of a century earlier (about 1520).

31. On the other hand, a letter from Michelangelo (Milanesi, p. 221) should be mentioned here, which he wrote to his nephew Lionardo in 1548, and in which he disassociated himself very emphatically from the Florentine *fuorusciti,* even denying that he had any relationship with them or had allowed himself to be looked after in Roberto Strozzi's house during his illness. He insisted that he was not living in the Strozzi house at that time but in Riccio's room (which, however, was located in Strozzi's house): ". . . mi son guardato insino a ora del parlare e praticare con fuorusciti . . . Circa l'essere stato amalato in casa gli Strozzi, io non tengo d'essere stato in casa loro, ma in camera di Messer Luigi del Riccio, il quale era molto mio amico . . ."

   In the years 1552 (Milanesi, p. 279) and 1553 (Milanesi, p. 289) Michelangelo repeated to his nephew the assertion that he had never remained in touch with the Florentine exiles. These letters are explained by Michelangelo's fear that his nephew, who was still in Florence, might be pestered by the Florentine authorities because of the well-known republicanism of his famous uncle. The letters should not mislead us, however, as to the true convictions of the artist.

32. Cf. Léon Dorez, *Bibliothèque de l'École des Chartes,* LXXVIII (1917), pp. 193 ff.

33. Cf. Tolnay, in *Jahrbuch der preussischen Kunstsammlungen,* LI (1930), pp. 22 ff., and LIII (1932), p. 239 ff. This is the first interpretation of the spiritual content of the Capitol, afterwards adopted by F. Saxl, *Lectures* (London, 1957), pp. 200 ff., and partly followed also by H. Siebenhüner, *Das Capitol in Rom* (Munich, 1954) and by Ackerman, *op. cit.* This is basically the idea of the Omphalos.

34. Cf. A. C. Soper, "The 'Dome of Heaven' in Asia," in *Art Bulletin* (1947), pp. 225 ff.; K. Lehmann, "The Dome of Heaven," *ibid.* (1945), pp. 1 ff.
   The church is a martyrium, erected above the tomb of St. Peter, and this fact partly explains why the new St. Peter's was conceived as a centrally planned building, i.e. as the martyria.

35. As the few original sketches by Michelangelo in Haarlem, Lille, Florence, and Oxford clearly show, the master wanted to raise the outer shell of the dome above a hemispherical shape, and in this Giacomo della Porta followed Michelangelo's intentions, although in a slightly exaggerated way, when he constructed the actual cupola. Concerning this much-debated problem, cf. the bibliographical references in Tolnay, *Encyclopedia universale dell'Arte,* Vol. IX (1963), pp. 298 ff. The problem will be discussed in greater detail in Tolnay VI.

36. Michelangelo is closer to the great allegorical frescoes of the end of the Middle Ages (e.g. Ambrogio Lorenzetti in the Palazzo Pubblico, Siena). The Italian municipali-

ties of the Middle Ages were fond of representing in large allegorical frescoes in their administrative palaces the true form of government, the *governo giusto* (or *buon governo*), that is the republican-democratic form, and contrasting it with representations of the bad form of government (*cattivo governo*), that is of tyranny. It is really this idea which Michelangelo adopted, except that in his *David* and *Hercules* he no longer represented the *governo giusto* by allegories but by the embodiment of spiritual powers in the form of biblical and mythological heroes, powers which are the basis of the republican form of government.

CHAPTER II

1.   Francesco Berni (cf. Frey, *Dicht.*, p. 263): "Ho visto qualche sue compositioni: Son' ignorante e pur direi l'haverle lette tutte nel mezo di Platone." [Condivi, ed. Frey, p. 204.] B. Varchi, *Due Lezzioni* (Florence, 1549), p. 52: ". . . tutti i componimenti di lui [*scil.* Michelangelo] [sono] pieni d'Amore Socratico, e di concetti Platonici . . ."

2.   Cf. H. Hettner, *Italienische Studien* (Braunschweig, 1879). V. Kaiser, "Der Platonismus Michelangelos," in *Zeitschrift für Völkerpsychologie und Sprachwissenschaft*, XV (1884), pp. 209 ff.; XVI (1886), pp. 138 ff. and 209 ff.

L. von Scheffler, *Michelangelo, eine Renaissance-Studie* (Altenburg, 1892).

H. Thode, *Michelangelo und das Ende der Renaissance* (Berlin, 1903), Vol. II, pp. 191 ff.

J. Oeri, "Hellenisches in der Medicikapelle," in *Baseler Nachrichten*, LXI (July 3, 1905).

K. Borinski, *Die Rätsel Michelangelos* (München,

1908). Tolnay, "Eine Sklavenskizze Michelangelos," in *Münchener Jahrbuch der Bildenden Kunst*, V (1928), pp. 70 ff. and the works cited in the following note; *idem.*, *L'Arte* (1934), pp. 5 ff. and 281 ff.; E. Panofsky, *Studies in Iconology* (New York, 1939), pp. 171 ff.

3. For a more detailed analysis of Michelangelo's works of art I shall take the liberty of referring to my own books in which I have tried to deal in greater detail with the philosophical aspects of the master's sculptures and frescoes. Cf. for the Ceiling of the Sistine Chapel: Tolnay, "La volta della Cappella Sistina," in *Bollettino d'Arte* (1936), and Tolnay II; for the Tomb of Julius II: *idem*, "Eine Sklavenskizze Michelangelos," in *Münchener Jahrbuch der Bildenden Kunst*, V (1928), pp. 70 ff., and Tolnay IV; for the Medici Chapel: *idem*, *L'Arte* (1934), pp. 5 ff and 281 ff., and Tolnay III; for the *Last Judgment*: *idem*, "Le Jugement Dernier de Michel-Ange," in *The Art Quarterly* (1940), pp. 125 ff., and Tolnay V.

4. Cf. Thode, *Michelangelo und das Ende der Renaissance* (Berlin, 1901), Vol. I, *passim;* Panofsky, *Studies in Iconology.*

5. Cf. Thode, *op. cit.*, and Panofsky, *op. cit.* above.

6. Varchi, *op. cit.*

7. The most important translations by Marsilio Ficino were those he made of the *Phaedrus*, the *Phaedo*, the *Philebus*, and the *Timaeus* by Plato; the *Enneads* by Plotinus (particularly Book I, Chapter 6, "On Beauty"; Book III, Chapter 5, "On Eros"; Book V, Chapter 8, "On Intelligible Beauty"); the *De Mysteriis* by Jamblicus; and the *De Anima et Daemone* by Proclus. Concerning Ficino, see the recent book by André Chastel, *Marsile Ficin et L'Art* (Geneva, 1954).

8. Cf. Tolnay I, pp. 75 f.

9. Cf. Tolnay I, pp. 99 f. The Virgin in the *tondo* made for Bartolommeo Pitti (Florence, Bargello) is similar.

10. All the Virgins which Michelangelo executed in his youth were made for private devotion and not for churches. In them Michelangelo transforms the traditional devotional images into an image for philosophical-religious meditation. They do not presuppose a devout believer in prayer, but rather a meditative spirit aspiring to philosophical consolation. It is a humanistic-religious conception.

11. The inspiration for this composition comes from Signorelli's *tondo* in the Uffizi where there are also nude youths, this time shepherds, in the background. Here too, the landscape of the background with its ancient triumphal arch has a pagan aspect.

12. Tolnay I, pp. 109 f.

13. Tolnay I, pp. 89 f.

14. Hence the so-called "Tragedy of the Tomb of Julius II" (Justi) which has been explained as being due to external difficulties or the master's lack of willpower because of an inner conflict between the project commissioned by the Pope and Michelangelo's own conception of the work. Cf. Tolnay IV.

15. Vasari, ed. Frey, pp. 67 f.; Condivi, p. 66.

16. The bottom zone in the first project for the Tomb of Julius II seems to have been identical with the bottom zone of the 1513 project, which later, about 1542, was executed in San Pietro in Vincoli. Cf. Tolnay, in *Münchener Jahrbuch* (1928), p. 420, note 39; E. Panofsky, *Art Bulletin*, XIX (1937), pp. 561 ff. I have attempted a reconstruction of the top zone of the 1505 version, on the basis of old paraphrases of the monument, in Tolnay IV.

17. Vasari calls the sarcophagus "bara," Condivi describes it

as "arca." The word *bara* has the meaning of "bier" and not of "sella gestatoria." It was erroneously argued that in this first project the Pope must have been sitting on the "sella" supported by two angels (Panofsky, *Art Bulletin* [1937], note 14). Other documents contradict this interpretation and demonstrate that Vasari used the word *bara* in its original sense, namely that of "sarcophagus" (cf. Tolnay IV).

18. Drawing in Berlin, Thode No. 5.
19. Cf. Tolnay, in *Münchener Jahrbuch* (1928), pp. 70 ff.
20. Panofsky, *Studies in Iconology,* pp. 192 ff.
21. In earlier similar Italian tombs there are generally only two zones, both signifying heaven: e.g. Matteo Civitale, monument of San Regulus, Lucca Cathedral.
22. For an interpretation of the whole Sistine Ceiling, cf. Tolnay II. My interpretation has been challenged by F. Hartt, *Art Bulletin* (1950), pp. 181 ff., and *idem, ibid.,* 1951, pp. 262 ff.; (cf. Tolnay's reply, *Art Bulletin* [1953], pp. 257 ff.); E. Wind, *Gazette des Beaux Arts* (1944), pp. 211 ff.; *idem, Measure,* 1950, pp. 411 ff.; in *Renaissance Studies* (1960), pp. 312 ff.; H. von Einem, *Michelangelo* (Stuttgart, 1959), pp. 51 ff. They believe that Michelangelo was inspired by theological writings: by Vigerio, according to Hartt; by Santo Pagnini, according to Wind; and by an anonymous source, according to von Einem. Consequently, in their opinion, the content of the cycle illustrates a theological program, in which the facts of the Old Testament serve as allusions to facts of the New Testament. But the simplicity of the general idea, namely the relationship between finite existences and infinite Existence, does not demand an erudite program; nor was it necessary to interpret the stories of the Ceiling typologically, since a typological relationship between the two Testaments

was already established in the two Quattrocento cycles on the walls below. The stories of the Ceiling do not allude to the future coming of Christ (Wind, *Art Bulletin* [1951], pp. 41 ff.), but reveal the presence of God. From the ideological point of view, as well as that of form, the Ceiling was conceived as an autonomous organism with respect to the rest of the Chapel.

Hartt and Wind, however, accept my interpretation of the close relationship between the seers and the adjacent histories, and also the sequence of the scenes from the entrance toward the altar.

23. After all, the Tomb of Julius II and the Medici Chapel have a similar structure. In all these works the universe is conceived as an "edifice," consisting of three superimposed zones: Hades, Earth, ὑπερουράνιος τόπος (instead of the Hell, Earth, and Paradise of the Middle Ages).

24. There was no fixed program for the Sistine Ceiling, as we know from a letter of Michelangelo himself (Milanesi, pp. 426 ff.). If I quote poets or philosophers of the Renaissance here, it is only in order to point out analogies between their works and that of Michelangelo, and not because I regard them as direct sources.

25. Cf. Tolnay II, *passim;* cf. also André Chastel, *Art et Humanisme à Florence*, 2nd ed. (Paris, 1958), who agrees with my views.

26. As in the cosmogonies of Hesiod and Lucian, Michelangelo seems to have believed that chaos existed first, and that God emerged from chaos. The cosmogony here includes the theogony as an organic part (cf. Tolnay II, p. 40).

27. These genii, projections of the threefold nature of the Prophets and Sibyls, should not be regarded as purely decorative figures.

28. For Nicholas of Cusa's conception of God, cf. E. Cassirer, *Individuum und Kosmos in der Philosophie der Renaissance* (Leipzig, 1927).

29. Similarly in Etruscan tombs the souls of the departed contemplate the divinities (Michel de Ferdinándy).

30. J. Oeri (*op. cit.*) was the first to notice the relationship between Plato's *Phaedo* and the ideas expressed in the Medici Chapel. But Oeri assumes these ideas to have been merely illustrated by Michelangelo and does not see the master's own contribution. My thesis of the syncretism between pagan and Christian concepts (cf. Tolnay, in *L'Arte* [1934], pp. 5 ff., pp. 281 ff.) has been adopted by Panofsky (*Studies in Iconology*) and extended to include the doctrine of the four temperaments. F. Hartt, in *Beiträge für Georg Swarzenski* (1951), pp. 145 ff., sees in the Chapel an allegory of the princely and papal power of the Medici and of their apotheosis, as do Vasari, Condivi, and Varchi (cf. Tolnay's reply in *Art Bulletin*, 1953, pp. 257 ff.). An interpretation based on the liturgy of the Requiem has been proposed by H. Brockhaus, *Michelangelo und die Medici Kappelle* (Leipzig, 1911), and by von Einem, *op. cit.*, pp. 82 ff. However, the conception of the survival of the soul and the beginning of a new life after death is as much pagan as Christian, and there is no contradiction in this matter between Plato's thoughts and the text of the Requiem.

31. Christ's gesture in the *Last Judgment* actually repeats the gesture of Jupiter in three drawings by Michelangelo, which represent the Fall of Phaeton and which were done before the *Last Judgment*. For these drawings cf. Tolnay III, pp. 111 ff. Cf. also some of the Resurrection drawings analyzed in Tolnay V.

32. For the conception of the *Sol Invictus* and the *Sol Justitiae*, cf. H. Usener, *Das Weihnachtsfest* (Bonn,

1911); E. Norden, "Die Geburt des Kindes," in *Studien der Bibliothek Warburg*, III (1924); F. Boll, *Die Sonne im Glauben und in der Weltanschauung der Völker* (Stuttgart, 1922); F. J. Dölger, *Sol Salutis* (Münster in Westphalen, 1925); L'Orange, *Constantiusbogen* (Oslo, 1935).

33. Cf. A. Warburg, *Gesammelte Schriften* (Leipzig, 1932).

34. The best analyses of the compositions of these two frescoes are in M. Dvořák, *Geschichte der italienischen Kunst* (Munich, 1928); cf. also Baumgart-Biagetti, *Die Fresken des Michelangelo in der Cappella Paolina* (Vatican City, 1934).

35. Cf. W. Windelband, *Geschichte der Philosophie*, 10th ed. (Tübingen, 1921); Cassirer, *op. cit.*

36. Cf. Tolnay, *Art Quarterly* (1940), pp. 125 ff.

37. Cf. also Michelangelo's letter of 1556 (Milanesi, p. 539) on the death of his servant Urbino: "[Urbino] morendo m'a insegnato morire, non con dispiacere, ma con desiderio della morte." ([Urbino] in dying has taught me how to die, not with displeasure, but with the desire for death.) Concerning Michelangelo's conception of death and resurrection, cf. Tolnay, "Morte e Resurrezzione in Michelangelo," *Commentari*, 1964/65 (in press).

38. Cf. *Dialoghi di Donato Giannotti*, ed. D. Redig de Campos (Florence, 1939), p. 69.

CHAPTER III

1. The theme of this chapter has been treated more than once, especially by H. Thode, *Michelangelo und das Ende der Renaissance*, Vol. II (Berlin, 1903), pp. 271 ff., and by Hermann Wolfgang Beyer, *Die Religion Michelangelos* (Bonn, 1926). These works do not, however,

try to define the special nature of Michelangelo's religious experience, nor to show the influence which this experience exercised on the iconography and style of his works.

Works on Michelangelo's religion from a purely Catholic point of view are: Sayn-Wittgenstein, *La Chapelle Sixtine* (Paris, 1867); J. Gava, "Michelangelos religiöses Glaubensbekenntnis," in *Historisch-Politische Blätter für das katholische Deutschland*, CXL (1907), pp. 81 and 175 ff.; M. Spahn, *Michelangelo und die Sixtinische Kapelle* (Berlin, 1907).

Works on Michelangelo's religiosity from a purely Protestant standpoint: M. Carrière, "Michelangelo und die Reformation," in *Zeitschrift für Bildende Kunst*, IV (1869), pp. 329 ff.; M. Dombre, *Étude sur la pensée religieuse de Michel-Ange* (Montauban, 1883); Hartmann, "Michelangelo als religiöser Charakter und evangelischer Zeuge," in *Deutsch-Evangelische Blätter*, XVI (1831), pp. 667 ff.; A. Revel, "La Mente di Michelangelo," in *Rivista Cristiana* (1875).

2. Cf. Milanesi, pp. 21, 33, 43.
3. Cf. Milanesi, pp. 205, 206, 211, 213, 222, 242, 244, 270, 272, 361.
4. The Virgin of the Bargello *tondo* is transformed into the Delphic Sibyl of the Sistine Ceiling.
5. The *putto* of the antique Phaedra-sarcophagus (called the sarcophagus of the Contessa Beatrice, Pisa, Camposanto) is transformed into the Jesus of the Bargello *tondo*.
6. The Christ of the *Last Judgment* is influenced by the Apollo Belvedere. The connection between Michelangelo's Virgin in the *Last Judgment* and the antique group of the Crouching Venus and Cupid was first pointed out by the late Gertrude Coor.

7. San Bernardino, *Le Prediche Volgari*, ed. L. Banchi (Siena, 1880), I (first sermon).

8. Savonarola, *Prediche sopra Job* (1494), No. 43 (Venice, 1545), pp. 374 ff. Cf. E. Steinmann, "Das Madonnenideal des Michelangelo," in *Zeitschrift für Bildende Kunst*, VII (1896), pp. 169 ff. and 201 ff.

9. Steinmann, *op. cit.*, on the other hand assumes a direct influence.

10. Condivi, ed. Frey, p. 204.

11. The letter of March 10, 1498 (Milanesi, p. 59), in which Savonarola is mentioned, is not, as has long been supposed, from Michelangelo, but from Piero d'Argiento, as G. Poggi, *Michelagniolo Buonarroti nel IV Centenario del Giudizio Universale* (Florence, 1942), pp. 113 ff., established; therefore it cannot be used as evidence.

12. The immediate reason for his departure for Rome was, according to Vasari and Condivi, the fact that the *Cupid* had been sold as an ancient statuette to Cardinal Riario in Rome, and Michelangelo had to clarify this affair.

13. "Eretico marcio," Milanesi, p. 59.

14. This manner of composing the Christ figure may have been partly determined by its location in the church.

15. Mention should be made here of a group of drawings (c. 1532–34) representing the Resurrected Christ, in which Christ appears beardless and naked like an ancient Apollo, directly anticipating the Christ-Judge of the *Last Judgment*. Concerning the dates and purposes of these drawings, cf. Tolnay V; *idem, Commentari*, 1964/65.

16. Two of these works came to light recently: a red chalk drawing of the Holy Family called *Il Silenzio* (Duke of Portland, England) published by Cecil Gould in *The Burlington Magazine* (1951), pp. 279 ff., and a badly preserved black chalk drawing of the *Pietà* (Isabella

Stewart Gardner Museum, Boston), published by Tolnay, *Record of the Art Museum of Princeton* (1953), pp. 44 ff. The rest are unfortunately lost and known only through copies.

17. About fifteen copies of this *Pietà* are known, which for the most part have been listed by H. Thode, *Michelangelo, Kritische Untersuchungen über seine Werke* (Berlin, 1908–13), Vol. II, pp. 492 ff. To this list several examples were added in Tolnay, article cited in the preceding note.

18. Cf. for example, the woodcut of the Holy Trinity by Dürer, 1511 (Bartsch, No. 122). An engraving by Agostino Veneto, after Andrea del Sarto (Bartsch, No. 40) of 1516, already shows the transformation of this type of Trinity into a Pietà, about thirty years before Michelangelo's *Pietà* for Vittoria Colonna. (Reproduced in F. Knapp, *A. del Sarto* [Leipzig, 1907], p. 31.)

19. The original of this composition has been lost; the best copies are in Windsor and in the British Museum in London.

20. This became the prototype for Mannerist and Baroque representations of the Crucifixion: for example, for El Greco, Guido Reni, Rubens, and Van Dyck.

21. The original, recently published by Cecil Gould in *The Burlington Magazine*, 1951, is in the collection of the Duke of Portland (cf. note 16 above).

22. From the literature on the Italian Reformation we cite the following works:
P. Chiminelli, *Scritti Religiosi dei Riformatori Italiani del '500* (Turin, 1925).
F. C. Church, *I Riformatori Italiani*, trans. D. Cantimori (Florence, 1933). With an extensive bibliography on this question in Vol. II, pp. 231 ff.

D. Cantimori, *Eretici Italiani del Cinquecento* (Florence, 1939).

Francesco Lemmi, *La Riforma in Italia* (Milan, 1939).

H. Jedin: *Geschichte des Konzils von Trient,* 2nd ed., Vol. I (Freiburg, 1951), Book I, Ch. 7.

Idem.: "Cardinal Contarini als Kontroverstheologe" in *Katholisches Leben und Kämpfe im Zeitalter der Glaubensspaltung* (1949).

Idem.: "Il Cardinal Pole e Vittoria Colonna" in *L'Italia Francescana 1947.*

Idem.: "Contarini und Camaldoli" in *Archivio Italiano per la Storia della Pietà,* Vol. II, 1953.

23. Cf. Valdés, *Diálogo de la Doctrina Cristiana,* publié par M. Bataillon (Coimbra, 1925).

24. Cf. E. Gothein, *Ignatius von Loyola* (Munich, n.d.).
Idem.: Reformation und Gegenreformation (Leipzig, 1924).

25. Cf. Ferrero and Muller, *Vittoria Colonna, Carteggio* (Turin, 1892), p. 232.

26. It is not known exactly when the friendship between Michelangelo and Vittoria Colonna began, but it could have started either in 1536 or in 1538. The latter date seems more plausible to me.

27. Milanesi, p. 514.

28. Cf. Jean Baruzi, *La Doctrine du Salut. Leçon professée au Collège de France* (Paris, 1927).

29. Cf. Gothein, *op. cit.*

30. The letter from Ochino to Vittoria Colonna is published by Ferrero and Muller, *op. cit.*

31. The letter of July 21, 1554, from Ignatius Loyola to Conde de Melito is published in *Cartas de San Ignacio de Loyola* IV (Madrid, 1887), pp. 228 f., and by A. E. Popp in *Münchener Jahrbuch* (1927), p. 419.

32. Cf. Popp., *op. cit.*, p. 418 (illustration).

33. Sonnet 365 by Petrarch runs thus:

> *I'vo piangendo i miei passati tempi*
> *I quai posi in amar cosa mortale,*
> *Senza levarmi a volo, abbiend'io l'ale*
> *Per dar forse di me non bassi exempi.*
> *Tu che vedi i miei mali indegni et empi,*
> *Re del cielo, invisibile, immortale,*
> *Soccorri a l'alma disviata e frale,*
> *E 'l suo defetto di tua grazia adempi;*
>
> . . . . . .
>
> *A quel poco di viver che m'avanza*
> *Et al morir, degni esser tua man presta!*
> *Tu sai ben che 'n altrui non ho speranza.*

34. Cf. in particular the representation of visions in certain miniatures of the end of the fourteenth and fifteenth centuries and later in the paintings of Tintoretto and El Greco.

35. For the dates suggested in the text, cf. Tolnay, *Repertorium für Kunstwissenschaft* (1927), p. 199, n. 2. Michelangelo intended to execute this composition (the Crucified Christ with Mary and John) in marble; a drawing by Michelangelo showing the marble block for this group is in the Archivio Buonarroti (published by Tolnay in *Münchener Jahrbuch*, p. 461, and Tolnay V).

36. However, this drawing was probably executed in 1558–59. Michelangelo had already worked (c. 1540), on an *Annunciation* which is known through copies (e.g. in the Lateran), but it was planned as a dramatic scene and not as the translation of a purely inner experience.

37. Originally the figure of this angel was drawn on the sheet in a standing position; only in a *pentimento* did

Michelangelo so change the position of the legs that the figure became a hovering one.

38. A *Deposition* by Fra Filippo Lippi in Cherbourg, Musée; cf. Pittaluga, *Filippo Lippi* (Florence, 1949), plate 137, and Tolnay V, illustration 372 shows a triangular composition with the same figures around the body of Christ. So this type must have been known in Tuscany before Michelangelo.

39. Cf. Tolnay, "The Rondanini Pietà," in *The Burlington Magazine*, LXV (1934), pp. 146 ff.; Baumgart, "Die Pietà Rondanini," in *Jahrbuch der preussischen Kunstsammlungen*, LII (1935), pp. 44 ff.; H. von Einem, "Bemerkungen zur Florentiner Pietà Michelangelos," in *Jahrbuch der preussischen Kunstsammlungen* (1940).

40. According to Francisco de Hollanda, *Four Dialogues on Painting*, ed. J. de Vasconcellos (Vienna, 1899), p. 109, Michelangelo is supposed to have said: "To represent adequately the face of the Savior is so difficult that it is not enough to be a great master with much knowledge. I am rather of the opinion that his life should be pure and if possible holy, so that the Holy Ghost may direct his thoughts."

CHAPTER IV

1. Condivi, ed. Frey, pp. 192 ff.: "Ingegnosa theorica, per lungo uso da lui ritrovata." "So bene, che quando legge Alberto Duro, gli par cosa molto debole . . . E a dire il vero, Alberto non tratta se non delle misure e varietà dei corpi, di che certa regula dar non si può, formando le figure ritte come pali; quel che più importava, degli atti e gesti humani, non ne dice parola."

The fact that Michelangelo intended to write a treatise on art is expressed by him also in Giannotti's

Dialoghi, p. 42, where he is presented as one of the interlocutors.

To complement this chapter, I refer the reader to the recently published and informative book by Robert J. Clements, *Michelangelo's Theory of Art* (New York, 1961). Clements treats the problem chiefly from the point of view of a historian of literature. Cf. also the review by Creighton Gilbert in *Art Bulletin* (1962), pp. 347, and Clements' reply in *ibid.*, (1963), pp. 173 ff.

2. Vincenzo Danti, *Il primo libro delle perfette proporzioni* (Florence, 1567). J. von Schlosser, in *Jahrbuch des Allerhöchsten Kaiserhauses*, XXXI (Vienna, 1913/14), pp. 81 ff., was the first to call attention to this little book. We used Danti to reconstruct Michelangelo's theory of art in "La Théorie d'Art et Michel-Ange," in *Deuxième Congrès International d'Esthètique et de Science de l'Art* (Paris, 1937), II, pp. 23 ff. Danti's treatise has recently been republished with critical notes by P. Barocchi in *Trattati d'Arte del Cinquecento* I (Bari, 1960), pp. 209 ff. and 494 ff. Professor Barocchi demonstrates among other things the influence of Aristotle's *Poetics* on Danti.

Some of the remarks in the *Dialogues* by Francisco de Hollanda seem also to revert to the master. My opinion concerning the partial—but only partial—reliability of de Hollanda is expressed in Tolnay V.

3. Cf. Lionello Venturi, *Histoire de la Critique d'Art* (Brussels, 1938). A. Blunt, *Artistic Theory in Italy* (Oxford, 1940). E. Battisti, "Il Concetto di imitazione nel Cinquecento da Raffaello a Michelangelo," in *Commentari* (1956), pp. 86 ff.

4. This principle, the so-called *perspective ralentie*, is treated in the recent book by Jurgis Baltrušaitis, *Anamorphoses ou perspectives curieuses* (Paris, 1955).

5. For the *Crucifix* cf. Tolnay I, pp. 195 ff. Recently this Crucifix was discovered by Dr. M. Lisner and published in *Kunstchronik* (January, 1963). Dr. Lisner is preparing a more detailed study to appear in *Münchener Jahrbuch*. I agree with her conclusions concerning the attribution to Michelangelo.

6. Condivi, ed. Frey, p. 194; cf. also Vasari, ed. Frey, p. 243. Realdo Colombo, *De re anatomica* (1559) contains observations which may be based on the exchange of opinions with Michelangelo.

7. Tolnay I, pp. 77 ff.

8. I discussed this more thoroughly in *Repertorium für Kunstwissenschaft*, XLVIII (1927), pp. 180 ff.

   There are a few anatomical drawings in red chalk, mainly in the Teyler Museum in Haarlem, in Windsor, and in the Casa Buonarroti in Florence, which have been attributed to Michelangelo; but these attributions are not entirely convincing.

9. Tolnay, *Repertorium*, XLVIII (1927), p. 179.

10. Benedetto Varchi, *Due Lezzioni* (Florence, 1549).

11. *Ghibertis Denkwürdigkeiten*, ed. von Schlosser (Berlin, 1912), p. 105.

12. Danti, *op. cit.*

13. P. Lomazzo, *Trattato dell'arte della Pittura*, Book IV, Ch. 7.

14. Vasari, ed. Frey, p. 244.

15. Varchi, *op. cit.*

16. Francisco de Hollanda, *Four Dialogues on Painting*, ed. J. de Vasconcellos (Vienna, 1899), pp. 29 ff.

17. Cf. Leonardo, *Trattato della Pittura*.

18. De Hollanda, *op. cit.*, pp. 29 ff.

19. Vasari speaks of idealized heads. In Michelangelo's work there are five self-portraits: one on the fresco *Judith and Holofernes* on the Sistine Ceiling (Tolnay II,

p. 95); another, in the *Last Judgment,* on the flayed skin of St. Bartholomew (La Cava, *Il Volto di Michelangelo* [Bologna, 1925]); a third, according to Vasari, is the face of Joseph of Arimathea in the *Deposition* in the Cathedral of Florence; a fourth is the head of St. Paul in the Piccolomini Altar, whose features also recall those of the master; and finally, the face of St. Paul in the *Conversion of St. Paul* in the Pauline Chapel may be considered as an idealized self-portrait of the master.

20. Niccolò Martelli, *Il primo libro delle Lettere di* N. M. (Florence, 1546), fol. 49 f.

21. R. W. Lee, "The Humanistic Theory of Painting," in *Art Bulletin,* XXII (1940), pp. 203 ff.

The story about the painter Zeuxis relates that when he made a painting representing Helen, or Venus according to some versions, for the temple near Croton, he did not have confidence in his own judgment, and so chose the five most beautiful virgins of the town, combining their best features in order to make his picture. The sources for this anecdote are Pliny, *Nat. Hist.* 36, 64, and Cicero, *De inventione rhetorica,* Book II, 1, par. 123. This story is already quoted in Alberti, *Della pittura,* ed. Janitschek, p. 51. Condivi asserts that Michelangelo also followed this selective method, whereas Danti (*ibidem,* Ch. XI, ed. Barocchi, p. 240) more judiciously states that: "Michelagniolo . . . s'avide molto bene questa strada non essere la vera e legitima . . ." (Michelangelo . . . realized very well that this path [i.e., the selective path] not being the true and legitimate one . . .)

Alongside the quattrocentesque doctrine of "exact imitation" of natural models, and the doctrine of "ideal imitation" based on the selection of the finest parts of several individuals to produce a more perfect figure, there is Michelangelo's conception, according to which visible nature should be surpassed through "the imitation of the intention of nature." This intention is actually the a priori inner idea or *concetto* in the spirit of the artist. Michelangelo emphasizes this innate idea when he says: "[Amore è] un concetto della belleza immaginata o vista dentro al core . . ." (Frey, *Dicht.* LX). ([Love is] a conception of beauty imagined or seen within the heart . . .)

This theory reverts to Ficino's Neo-Platonic doctrine (cf. André Chastel, *Marsile Ficin et l'Art* [Geneva, 1954], p. 72), and became the source of the mannerist theory of the *disegno interno*.

Mention may be made here of the empirical definition of Beauty as the effect of "una certa grazia," sustained by Michelangelo's contemporary B. Varchi, *Libro della beltà e grazia* (cf. Barocchi, *Trattati d'Arte del Cinquecento* [1960], pp. 85 ff.).

22. The testimony of these two contemporaries clearly shows that the *non finito* was appreciated in Michelangelo's time, and refutes the widespread opinion of some recent scholars that this appreciation begins only with the Romantic period.

Even more explicit concerning the value of the unfinished is Bocchi-Cinelli (1677, pp. 138 f.) in the following sentence about the Boboli Slaves: ". . . con lo scarpello, e con la mano anzi con la gradina rozzamente [ha] cavati dal sasso corpi umani, i quali non finiti, ne equivochi, ma naturali, e veri si dimostrano. E di vero più sono queste statue maravigliose in questa guisa, che se del tutto fossero compiute . . ." (. . . human bodies which [he] has carved with the chisel, and with the hand, and even roughly carved with the tooth chisel, although unfinished show themselves not as equivocal but as natural and true, and indeed these statues are more marvelous in this state than if they were completely finished . . .). I called attention to this important passage in Tolnay III and Tolnay IV, pp. 62 f., on which is based also the article by André Chastel, "Le fragmentaire, l'hybride et l'inachevé," published in *Das Unvollendete als künstlerische Form* (Bern, 1959), pp. 83 ff. Concerning Vasari's sentences about the value of the unfinished, already quoted by me in the German edition (1948) of this book, see now Gantner, *Rodin und Michelangelo* (Vienna, 1953), p. 45.

23. Aldo Bertini, "Il problema del non finito nell' arte di Michelangelo," in *L'Arte*, XXXIII (1930), pp. 121 ff. Cf. also the recent publication of A. Stoke, *Michelangelo: A Study in the Nature of Art* (London, 1955) and *Das Unvollendete als künstlerische Form*, J. A. Schmoll (Eisenwerth) (Bern, 1959), which contains important articles relating to this problem.

24. The *Battle of the Centaurs* always remained in Michelangelo's workshop (Vasari). Since it is small, it would have been an easy matter to finish it; therefore the fact that Michelangelo left it roughhewn indicates that he was satisfied with it in this state.

25. Cf. E. Panofsky, *Idea* (Leipzig, 1924), p. 65.

26. Cf. the analysis in Tolnay II.

27. Cf. J. Wilde, "Der ursprüngliche Plan Michelangelos zum Jüngsten Gericht," in *Die Graphischen Künste* (Vienna, N. F. I, 1963), pp. 7 ff.

28. Cf. for example the *St. Matthew* in the Academy of Florence. For Michelangelo's creative principles and his marble technique, see the contributions by E. Guillaume, "Michel-Ange Sculpteur" in *Gazette des Beaux Arts* (1876), p. 34 ff.; E. Löwy, "Stein und Erz," in *Kunstgeschichtliche Anzeigen*, XXXVI (Vienna, 1915),

pp. 5 ff.; and A. Grünwald, *Florentiner Studien* (Prague, 1914).

29. So the unpolished surfaces in the master's last works are not the result of carelessness nor do they signify for him that the works were unfinished.

30. For the Gothic elements in these last works cf. Tolnay, *Repertorium für Kunstwissenschaft* (1927), pp. 202 ff. Gothic features appear in Michelangelo's art as early as the *Pietà* of St. Peter's. The 1513 version of the upper zone of the Tomb of Julius II is in its verticalism and tension probably also inspired by Gothic architecture. The use of the orders as an architectural skeleton, where columns or pilasters have the function of buttresses, is structurally Gothic too, although clothed in classical forms. Examples are the Ricetto of the Laurentian Library, the Palazzo de' Conservatori, and the new St. Peter's.

31. Michelangelo's Ganymede composition is inspired by an ancient prototype, of which there are copies in Sussa for example, cf.: *Art Bulletin* (1960), pp. 246 ff. He characteristically altered it slightly to make it into a more expressive image of his love passion. The drawing published here is a contemporary copy, now in the Fogg Museum of Art, Cambridge, Mass.

32. For a more detailed treatment of Michelangelo's Resurrection drawings, cf. Tolnay, "Morte e Resurrezione in Michelangelo," *Commentari*, 1964/65 (in press).

33. Milanesi, p. 225: "Al Prete dì' che non mi scriva più a Michelagniolo Scultore, perchè io non ci son conosciuto se non per Michelagniolo Buonarroti, e che se un cittadino fiorentino vuol far dipigniere una tavola da altare, che bisognia che e' truovi un dipintore: chè io non fu' mai pittore ne scultore, come chi ne fa bottega. Sempre me ne son guardato per l'onore di mio padre e de' mia frate-

(141)

PLATE XLI

gli, ben io abbi servito tre Papi: chè è stato forza."
(Say to the priest that he should no longer address me
as Michelagniolo Scultore, because I am not known here
except as Michelagniolo Buonarroti, and if a Florentine
citizen wants to have an altar panel painted, then he
must find a painter, because I never was a painter nor a
sculptor who keeps a shop. I have always guarded
against that for the honor of my father and my brothers,
although I have served three popes: which I did under
duress.)

34. For the new concept of the artist held by Alberti and
Leonardo cf. the penetrating remarks in E. Cassirer, *Individuum und Kosmos in der Philosophie der Renaissance* (Leipzig, 1927), which I have used in the text.
However, Cassirer does not speak of the new concept of
the artist held by Michelangelo.

Excerpt from the Preface to the

Lectures at the Collège de France, 1948

I AM most appreciative of the honor bestowed on me by the Collège de France in inviting me to speak within its halls on the art and thought of Michelangelo. My thanks are due to the Administrator and professors who were kind enough to approve the invitation. I would like to express my gratitude in particular to my illustrious friend Monsieur Jean Baruzi who first suggested it.

It is a high honor to speak about the great Florentine master in the Collège de France, because its founder was one of Michelangelo's ardent admirers during the latter's lifetime.

Several times Francis I made known to Michelangelo his great desire to have one of the master's works for his collection. He did succeed in acquiring the *Hercules*, a copy of the *Leda*, and molds of the *Christ of the Minerva*, and of the *Pietà* in St. Peter's; later he received as a gift the *Slaves* from the Tomb of Julius II, which are now in the Louvre. Furthermore, the King tried hard to attract the master to his court. The most propitious moment came in 1529, when the Florentine Republic was endangered. Shortly before the siege, Michelangelo had fled to Venice; from there he intended to go on to France. At the time the King made generous offers. But the royal message arrived in Venice too late. Michelangelo had in the meantime gone back to Florence.[1]

Quite apart from this, the scientific study of Michelangelo in the Collège de France has a tradition which is already three-quarters of a century old. It goes back to the first holder of the Chair of Aesthetics and the History of Art, Charles Blanc (1878–82), a connoisseur of Michelangelo's art and author of a monograph on the subject. His successor, Eugène Guillaume (1882–83), himself a sculptor, wrote an article on "Michelangelo as Sculptor," a study which ranks among the most notable nineteenth-century works on Michelangelo. The last occupant of the Chair, Henri Focillon, in his fine book on Raphael touched several times on the subject of this book. He used Michelangelo mainly as a contrast to Raphael, evoking in a few powerful strokes the "bitter" side of his art, his customary vehemence and resentment, and contrasting them with the more tender humanity of Raphael."[2]

[1] Concerning the relationship between Francis I and Michelangelo, cf., in particular, Léon Dorez, Bibliothèque de l'École des Chartes, LXXXVIII (1917), pp. 193 ff.

[2] Cf. Charles Blanc, "Michel-Ange Buonarroti," in Histoire des Peintres de Toutes les Écoles (Paris, 1876); idem., "Le Génie de Michel-Ange dans le Dessin," in Gazette des Beaux Arts, XIII, 2 (1876), pp. 5 ff. Eugène Guillaume, "Michel-Ange, Sculpteur," in G. d. B. A., XIII, 2 (1876), pp. 34 ff. This article is one of the most important contributions of the nineteenth century for an analysis of Michelangelo's sculptural technique. Guillaume is, after Delacroix, the first of the modern authors to have recognized the positive value of the "unfinished" in Michelangelo's statues.

Due to the initative of Blanc and Guillaume, a volume of French scholarly articles was published on the occasion of the fourth centenary of Michelangelo's birth (Paris, 1876).

H. Focillon, Raphael (Paris, 1926).

ILLUSTRATIONS

MICHELANGELO: *The Virgin of the Steps*. Florence, Casa Buonarroti

MICHELANGELO: *The Battle of the Centaurs*. Florence, Casa Buonarroti

MICHELANGELO:
The Pietà of St. Peter's

MICHELANGELO:
The Virgin of Bruges.
Bruges,
Church of Notre-Dame

MICHELANGELO: *The Tondo of Bartolommeo Pitti*. Florence, Museo Nazionale

MICHELANGELO:
The Tondo of Taddeo Taddei.
London, Royal Academy

MICHELANGELO:
The Virgin of Angelo Doni.
Tempera on wood. Florence, Uffizi

BASTIANO DA SANGALLO: Copy after Michelangelo's *Battle of Cascina*, grisaille.
Lord Leicester, Holkham, England

MICHELANGELO: *St. Proculus.*
Bologna, San Domenico

MICHELANGELO: *St. Petronius.*
Bologna, San Domenico

RUBENS: Copy after Michelangelo's lost *Hercules*. Paris, Louvre

MICHELANGELO: *Bacchus*.
Florence, Museo Nazionale

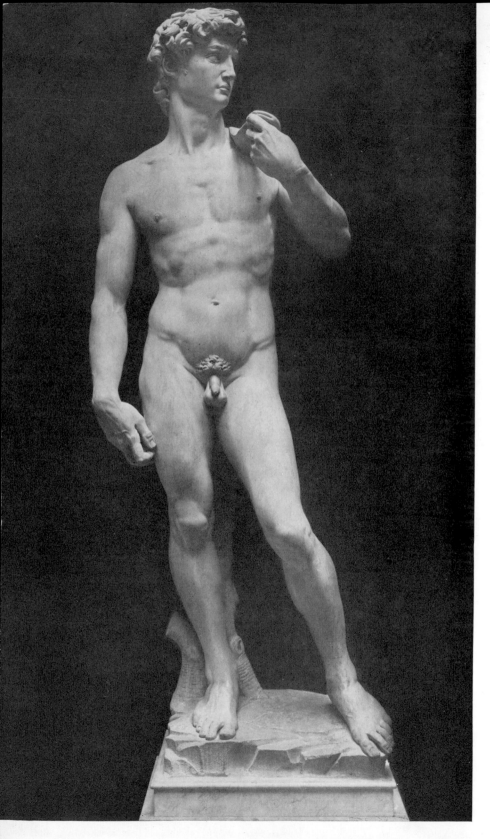

MICHELANGELO: *David*. Florence, Academy

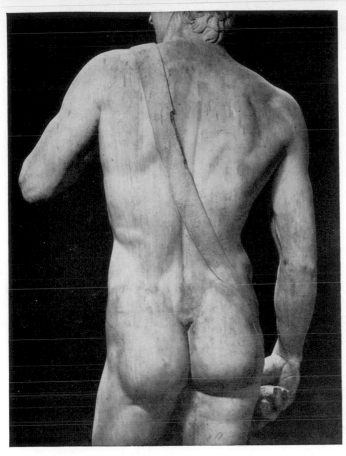

MICHELANGELO: *David, detail of the back.*
Florence, Academy

MICHELANGELO: *St. Matthew.* Florence, Academy

MICHELANGELO: *The Delphic Sibyl.*
Vatican, Sistine Chapel

MICHELANGELO: *The Prophet Isaiah.*
Vatican, Sistine Chapel

MICHELANGELO: *The Dying Slave.*
Paris, Louvre

MICHELANGELO: *The Rebellious Slave.*
Paris, Louvre

MICHELANGELO: *Moses.*
Rome, San Pietro in Vincoli

MICHELANGELO: *The Christ-Judge,*
detail from *The Last Judgment*

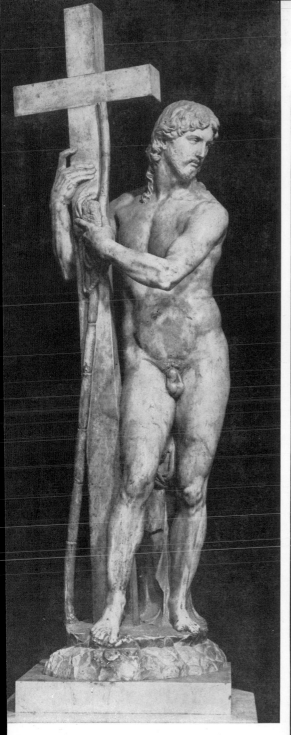

MICHELANGELO: *Christ with the Cross.*
Rome, Santa Maria sopra Minerva

MICHELANGELO:
The Tomb of Duke Lorenzo de' Me
Florence, Medici Chapel

MICHELANGELO:
The Tomb of
Duke Giuliano de' Medici.
Florence, Medici Chapel

MICHELANGELO: *The Medici Virgin*. Florence, Medici Chapel

MICHELANGELO: *The Victory*. Florence, Palazzo Vecchio

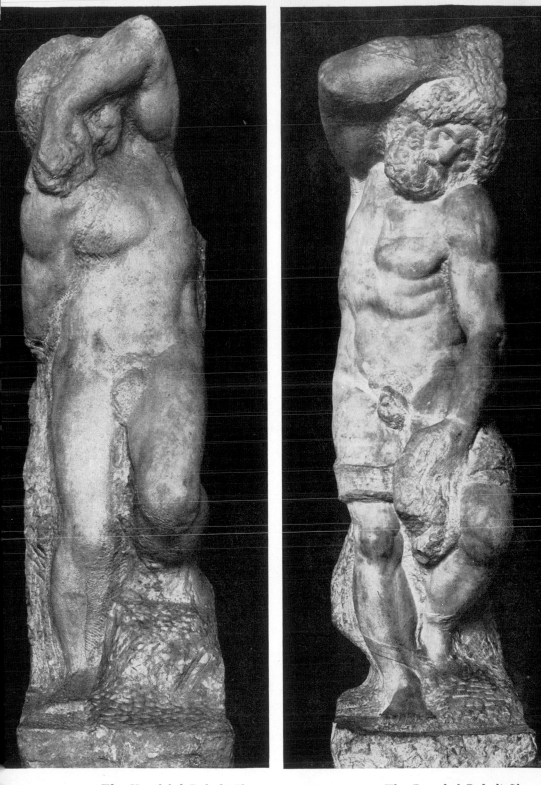

MICHELANGELO: *The Youthful Boboli Slave.*
Florence, Academy

MICHELANGELO: *The Bearded Boboli Slave.*
Florence, Academy

MICHELANGELO:
The so-called Atlas Boboli Slave.
Florence, Academy

MICHELANGELO:
The Awakening Boboli Slave.
Florence, Academy

MICHELANGELO: *Rachel.*
Rome, San Pietro in Vincoli

MICHELANGELO: *Leah.*
Rome, San Pietro in Vincoli

MICHELANGELO: *The Deposition,* also called *The Pietà.*
Florence, Santa Maria del Fiore

MICHELANGELO: *The Pietà Rondanini.* Milan, Castello Sforzesc

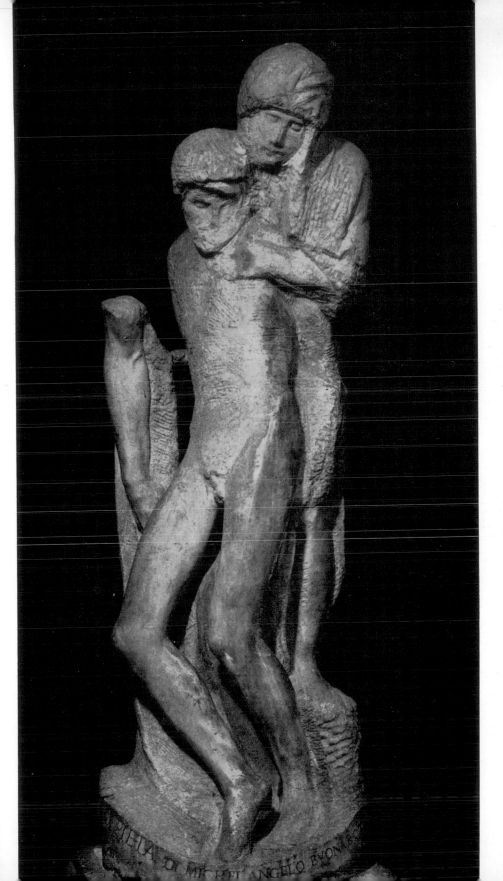

OPERA DI MICHELANGELO BVONARROTI

MICHELANGELO:
Head of the Virgin of Bruges.
Bruges, Notre-Dame

MICHELANGELO:
*Head of the Virgin from
the Bartolommeo Pitti Tondo.*
Florence, Museo Nazionale

MICHELANGELO: *Head of St. Proculus.*
Bologna, San Domenico

MICHELANGELO: *Head of David.* Florence, Academy

MICHELANGELO:
*Head of St. Paul from the
Piccolomini Altar.*
Siena, Cathedral

MICHELANGELO:
Head of Moses.
Rome, San Pietro in Vincoli

MICHELANGELO:
Head of Duke Lorenzo de' Medici
Florence, Medici Chapel

MICHELANGELO: *Head of Duke Giuliano de' Medici.*
Florence, Medici Chapel

MICHELANGELO: *Head of Brutus*. Florence, Museo Nazionale

MICHELANGELO:
Fibula from the Brutus Bust.
Florence, Museo Nazionale

MICHELANGELO:
Head of Joseph of Arimathea,
detail of *The Deposition.*
Florence, Santa Maria del Fiore

MICHELANGELO:
Heads of Christ and the Virgin
from the Pietà Rondanini.
Milan, Castello Sforzesco

Tomb of St. Dominic.
Bologna, San Domenico

Reconstruction of the first version
of the Tomb of Julius II
by Charles de Tolnay
(designed by Denise Fossard)

JACOMO ROCCHETTI: Copy of the second version
of the Tomb of Julius II, 1513.
Berlin, Kupferstich Kabinett

MICHELANGELO:
The Tomb of Julius II.
Rome, San Pietro in Vincoli

MICHELANGELO: *The Sistine Ceiling.* Vatican, Sistine Chapel

MICHELANGELO: *The Creation of Eve*. Vatican, Sistine Chapel

MICHELANGELO: *The Creation of Adam*. Vatican, Sistine Chapel

MICHELANGELO: *God Separating Water and Earth*. Vatican, Sistine Chapel

MICHELANGELO: *God Separating Light and Darkness*. Vatican, Sistine Chapel

MICHELANGELO: *The Medici Chapel.* Florence, San Lorenzo

MICHELANGELO: *Lateral walls of the Medici Chapel.* Florence, San Lorenzo

MICHELANGELO: *The Last Judgment*. Vatican, Sistine Chapel

MICHELANGELO: *The Conversion of St. Paul.* Vatican, Pauline Chapel

MICHELANGELO: *The Crucifixion of* St. Peter. Vatican, Pauline Chapel

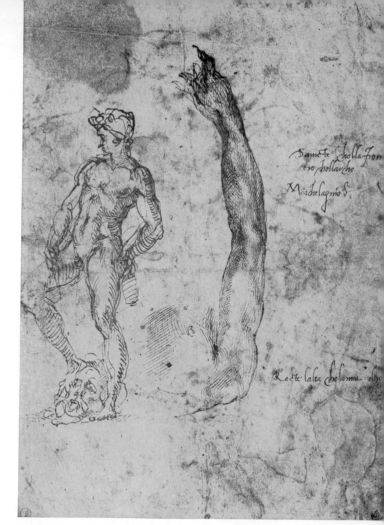

MICHELANGELO:
Sketch for the Bronze David.
Pen and ink. Paris, Louvre

MICHELANGELO:
Sketches of Four Masks
and
Sketch for the Hercules
and Antaeus. Red chalk
London, British Museum

MICHELANGELO: *Sketch for the Resurrection of Christ.* Red chalk. Paris, Louvre.

MICHELANGELO: *The Resurrection of Christ, second version.* Black chalk. Windsor Castle, Royal Library

MICHELANGELO:
The Resurrection of Chris
Black chalk.
London, British Museum

MICHELANGELO:
The Fall of Phaeton.
Black chalk.
London, British Museum

Copy after
Michelangelo's *Ganymede*.
Black chalk.
Cambridge, Mass.,
Fogg Museum of Art

MICHELANGELO: *Tityus*. Black chalk. Windsor Castle, Royal Library

ATTRIBUTED TO MICHELANGELO:
Christ on the Cross,
made for Vittoria Colonna.
Black chalk.
London, British Museum

MICHELANGELO:
Sketch of a leg.
Black chalk.
Vatican Library,
Cod. Vat. 3211, fol. 93 verso

MICHELANGELO:
Madonna del Silenzio.
Red chalk. Collection of the
Duke of Portland, England

MICHELANGELO:
Pietà, made for Vittoria Colonna
Black chalk. Boston,
Isabella Stewart Gardner Museum

MICHELANGELO:
*Christ on the Cross
with the Two Centurions.*
Black chalk.
Oxford, Ashmolean Museum

MICHELANGELO:
*Christ on the Cross
with the Virgin and St. John.*
Black chalk.
London, British Museum

MICHELANGELO: *The Annunciation*. Black chalk. Oxford, Ashmolean Museum

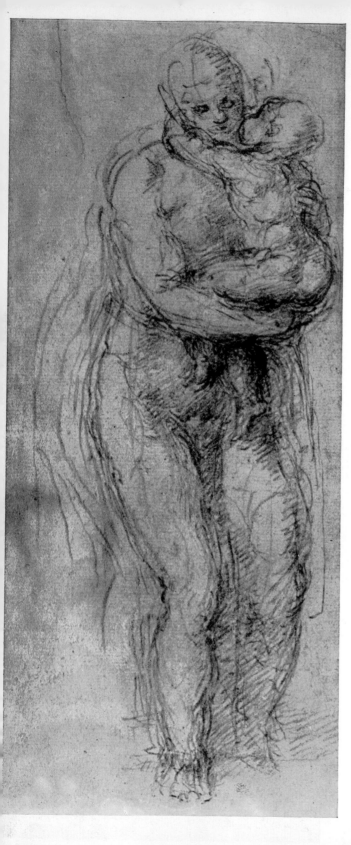

MICHELANGELO:
Virgin and Child.
Black chalk.
London, British Museum

DONATELLO: *St. George.*
Florence, Museo Nazionale

DONATELLO: *The Bronze David.*
Florence, Museo Nazionale

*Detail from an
ancient Hercules Sarcophagus.*
Rome, Museo delle Terme

OMENICO AND DAVID GHIRLANDAIO:
*The David above the
Cappella Sassetti.*
Florence, Santa Trinità

MICHELANGELO: *Three Menus.*
Florence, Archivio Buonarroti,
Cod. X, fol. 578

DANIELE DA VOLTERRA:
Portrait of Michelangelo.
Black chalk.
Haarlem, Teyler Museum